W9-CHM-155

FEROCIOUS IRISH WOMEN

FEROCIOUS IRISH WOMEN

Edmund Lenihan

THE MERCIER PRESS

The Mercier Press, 4 Bridge Street, Cork
24 Lower Abbey Street, Dublin 1

© Edmund Lenihan 1991

ISBN 0 85342 977 4

A CIP record for this book is available from the British Library.

To Mary,

the most ferocious of them all

Printed in Ireland by Colour Books Ltd.

Contents

Acknowledgements

My thanks to Gearóid Ó Crualaoich, UCC, for his expert and generous advice on Irish folk tradition. Without his guidance I would have made far more mistakes than I have. Thanks also to Kathleen Hegarty and Geraldine Hyland of Roscommon library for information on Lady Betty, to the staff of Kilkenny library for sending material on Alice Kyteler my way, to Mary Moroney of the local history section of Clare County Library, and finally to Cathal and Eoin, whose insatiable nightly demands for new stories forced me on even when I felt that I could do no more.

Míle buíochas dóibh go léir.

Introduction

In our time, when attention is being paid to more aspects of women as individuals and to their role in society than heretofore, it may be appropriate to pause a moment and question the generally-held view that women in previous ages were voiceless, subservient creatures merely, part of that silent, anonymous mass of humanity that has had precious few chroniclers.

In Ireland we are fortunate to possess both literary and oral accounts ('stories' as I will call them) of women through the centuries that by no means conform to this widely-held notion. As in other societies, our male ancestors understood well enough that women were as important and necessary in the scheme of things as themselves. This may have been given little political expression but in their stories (the then version of what we call 'history') it was allowed more scope. Thus we have in the cycle of mythological tales supernatural figures such as the sovereignty queen, who in folk tradition is represented as the banshee. Aoibheall, protector of the O'Brien clan, is one such, and though she is far removed in origin from mortal men, yet her behaviour at times of family crisis lends her a most palpable humanity. Warning she brings, certainly, but also a promise of comfort, so long as her advice is heeded.

The price of ignoring her counsel is demonstrated clearly by what happens to Dúlaing Ó hArtagáin, a chieftain of some sensibility, who is called on to perform a warrior's distasteful duty at Clontarf in the fateful year 1014. Before the battle he is allowed by Aoibheall what is seldom granted in this world: a view of the outcome, and a means of avoiding its worst effects. But what man will be said by a mere woman, especially when faced with the mockery of his male companions? He casts aside her advice and pays the ultimate price, neither the first nor the last to do so.

But it is not only as banshee or goddess that the sovereignty queen is represented in Irish tradition. Sometimes she appears also as the loathsome hag and motifs from the Goddess-cum-Hag domain inform of many female roles both in story and in life. In the latter category, for example, wise women (*mná feasa*), midwives (*mná ghlúine*) and keeners (*mná chaointe*) drew on aspects of the goddess in their performances, and were respected accordingly.

In County Clare there is no better candidate for the dubious title of hag than Máire Rua (Red Mary) McMahon. Yet, the disgust is tempered by a healthy respect, for she was that rare thing: a most feminine woman who yet succeeded in taking upon herself the role of the male hero. Her marriages to a succession of 'warriors' and her victory over each is very definitely a feature of the sovereignty queen myth — as is what she developed into in her later years: a virago, feared and avoided because of her exactions and depredations — in short, a gruesome hag. Even the Parliamentary General Ireton could make no hand of her. Yet a strange figure, the old blind man known as Maistín Caoch na Cruaiche, held her power in check and she was finally brought to ruin by nothing stronger than the curse of a poor widow whom she had tried to dispossess. An ironic end, certainly, to one whose abilities augured so well for her fortunes, and evidence that the flesh-and-blood origin of Máire was no proof against the supernatural magic of the widow's curse.

Another who aspired to maleness was Lady Betty, the Roscommon hangwoman, though, as in the case of Máire Rua, her success brought her little public approval and even less posthumous affection. Thrown on the mercies of the open road with a young family in eighteenth century Ireland, her very survival hung by a thread. But survive she did, a strange mixture of hard exterior and doting reliance on her one remaining son. When he eventually escaped from her smothering embrace her mind almost turned and she became a bitter old recluse, avoided by all.

The son's return years later, her failure to recognise him, her brutal murder of him for his money: this is the very stuff of tragedy — or of melodrama. But it is the strange aftermath that has held the eye of memory ever since — her discovery, condemnation and reprieve from the gallows on her volunteering to perform the duties of the absent hangman. And how lovingly she performed her grisly work is attested to by the abrupt fall in the crime rate for the area under her control.

Nor did she mellow with the passage of time; rather she secured for herself a sinister niche in the lore of that part of Ireland and died peacefully years later in her bed. But even yet in Roscommon, sight of the old jail — converted to more humane uses now, but still gaunt and secretive — provokes a shudder in many a passer-by, and on moonless nights, they say, the vain whimperings of those doomed to face Betty's calloused hands on the morrow can still occasionally be heard.

Similar to Lady Betty, but with an added otherworldly dimension, is the infamous Moll Shaughnessy, or *Spioraid na mBearnan* as she is better known in the borderlands between west Limerick and Kerry. Latterly a terrifying spectre to all foolish enough to pass the lonesome heights of Barna by night, she began life as the beautiful daughter of a poor tenant-farmer. Unwilling to be a burden to her parents, she chose her own husband, a rich but disfigured man. And a disastrous choice he turned out to be. Each time he looked at his new bride the contrast between his own ugliness and her beauty seemed to him more pronounced. His manner, as well as his habits, soon changed for the worse. Drink, arguments, finally beatings, drove Moll to desperation until at last she could take no more. On an evil day she buried the poker between his eyes and, aghast at what she had done, at once set about disposing of the body, piece by piece.

Shortly thereafter the guardians of the law arrived with their bloodhounds and almost by accident discovered part of the husband's remains. Moll was arrested and justice inexorably took its course. She was condemned, sentenced and hanged in her own yard at Barna.

Yet her story was merely beginning, for from that time on, an evil presence began to haunt the road that meanders up the hill. By fall of dark every traveller would make haste to be well clear of the place, leaving it to its spectral visitor. And so things stood for generations, until one night in November a poor cobbler, distraught at his wife's illness, rode madly that way in search of a doctor — only to feel icy fingers on his windpipe as he plunged down the fatal hillside! Struggle he did, like a madman, but in vain. With death staring him in the face, he begged for mercy — for his wife, if not for himself. And lo! Some nerve of compassion was touched in the fearsome creature. She released him, with the warning: 'Go, get the doctor for your wife, but be back here to me this night week.'

Worried to his wits' end he consulted his parish priest, and armed at last with that worthy man's advice, he returned to Barna at the time appointed. A battle royal followed, but the holy man's power — praise be the Lord! — was not to be gainsaid, and the unhallowed thing was banished at last, into the depths of Lough Gur, where she remains to this day.

Last of all the characters whose story is recounted in this collection, Alice Kyteler, the so-called Kilkenny witch, is of a different tradition than the others. That she is remembered as a witch — and was tried and convicted of witchcraft — should alert us to the kind of society to which she belonged: the Anglo-Norman culture of the fourteenth century Pale. Among such people — mainly English and Welsh settlers — witchcraft was a fact of life, a certain proof that the Devil is active in the world and freely abetted by misguided men and women. Like some perennial weed it is liable to spring up in the most unexpected of places, therefore the gardener had need to be extra vigilant to retard its progress. Or so went the thinking of the Church, the gardener-in-chief.

It is now not possible, almost seven centuries later, to

say with any certainty how justified the authorities were in bringing charges of witchcraft against Dame Kyteler, but it seems reasonably clear that there were motives other than righteous indignation at work in the case — motives such as jealousy, greed and a deal of political intrigue. For Alice had much to lose by being convicted; her people were bankers, after all. Yet, though she was found guilty of the preferred charges she does not seem to have suffered the utmost rigours of the law. That fate was, as so often, endured only by the lesser actors in the drama, such as Petronilla de Meath, her servant-woman. Alice, ever elusive, slipped from history without trace. Some say that friends spirited her away to England. Others maintain that the Devil spirited her to quite a different place! One way or another, it seems hardly likely that we will ever know for certain, and this — the unknown — is surely part of her abiding attraction.

EDMUND LENIHAN

1

AOIBHEALL
THE BANSHEE

In Ireland long ago every family that had the least pretension to respectability had a banshee of its own. Without one its members would be regarded as not Irish at all, only upstarts, vagabonds and 'sprus'.

Now, the men of Dál gCais, the Dalcassians, were different from most other Irish clans in one thing: they took immense pride in the fact that their banshee was one of the handful of such spirit women in all of Ireland whose name was known. It had been discovered, so family tradition had it, in the distant past by Seanchán, one of their most powerful druids, but so many generations had in the meantime passed away that though she was universally respected, even feared, among them there was now no agreement on what the original form of that name had been when the minds of men were undimmed by the pettinesses of everyday living. Aoibheall some called her. Others, in the best Clare fashion, refused to accept that. 'No,' they said. 'That isn't it, at all! Her right name is Aoibhinn, the Lovely One.' Maybe they were merely trying to keep on the right side of her, for she was one who had many unearthly powers and was not at all loath to invoke them against those whom she judged to have injured her good repute within the clan. Also, since she was a sister of the terrible Áine, whose fairy palace was at Knockainey in County Limerick, there was a double incentive to speak well of her.

It was she who, in withered and ancient form, led the twenty-five banshees of Clare to Rath Lake the night before the Battle of Dysert O'Dea in July of 1318. Imagine the shock to Richard de Clare, that proud, fearless Norman lord, whose intent was to snatch for himself the lands of Inchi-

13

quin, when he and his men came on these haggish women just before dawn, scrubbing rich robes and armour till the water boiled and ran red with blood! He recovered himself quickly, though.

'Out of our way, filthy crones, or by God's bones we'll trample ye.'

They ignored him, as if he and his army were mere shadows. Incredulous, he halted his progress. Accustomed to having his every whim obeyed without question, he could only stare at these weird figures and their frantic labours. His next words, when they came, were an anti-climax, almost forlorn: 'What devilment are ye doing there, anyway?'

Aoibheall it was who approached him with his answer, seeming to reach it to him with the dishevelled garments she offered.

'Washing *your* clothes and the clothes of your men. Hah-haaaaah!' Her laugh chilled them to the bone, far more intensely than the early coolness of that fatal day. Aghast, they stood transfixed as the terrible figures slowly dissolved into the lakeside mist, and many a flinty warrior, men who had faced Turks and heathen hordes unafraid, threw furtive glances towards their leader then. We will never know what De Clare thought, whether he hesitated in face of this evil omen, for at that moment a messenger tore up, gasped out his news — that the Irish forces were mustering on the Hill of Scool and haste was of the essence. In the flurry which followed to reach high ground at Tullyodea, to the north-east, the warning of Aoibheall was forgotten, and so it came to pass that later in the day, his customary arrogance now in full flow again, he forced a passage of the little stream at Macken Bridge but was ambushed a short distance away and cut down, together with several of his chief commanders. Thus began a rout, which developed into a bloody massacre. The bodies of De Clare's Normans and their Irish allies were scattered for miles and only a battered and scarred remnant reached the relative safety of Bunratty castle — relative, because less than a week later De Clare's widow, in her despair and anguish, burned it and set sail down the Shannon for England, never again to see the land of which her husband had intended her to be mistress.

That was but one example of the power of Aoibheall. Three hundred years earlier, in the days when Brian Boru was busily trying to convince the chiefs of Ireland that he was their High King and ought to be treated as such, she made her presence felt also. In the year of destiny, 1014, the Danes of Dublin, anxious to control all of Ireland within the four seas and to be rid of the threat of this Dalcassian upstart, invited their cousins in Man and Lochlainn to help them share the spoils. Brian's spies quickly informed him of what was afoot and he sent out speedy messengers to all parts of his domain to collect the royal levies. In their thousands they came, the fighting-men of the south-west, and gathered near the royal palace of Kincora, at the southern end of Lough Derg, where they were welcomed, every one, by Murrough, eldest son of the king. That evening, as the campfires began to be lit, Brian summoned the chieftains to the royal enclosure; there were plans to be laid, strategies to be defined, and jealousies to be allayed — for Brian well knew that it was such petty spites and hatreds, so common among the Irish, that had allowed the Northmen to gain first a foothold, then finally loom so menacing over the entire land. Every man of those touchy chiefs was carefully allotted his appropriate place, therefore, at the royal table.

But when all were seated, Murrough noticed that one place was empty. He thought for a moment, glanced swiftly about again to make doubly sure of his man, then hurried to Brian, whispered in the royal ear:

'Father,' he said, 'where is Dúlaing Ó hArtagáin? I don't see him.'

'Was he sent for?' asked Brian.

'Wasn't everyone sent for?'

'*In ainm Dé*, son, don't worry your head about him. We

have more to be thinking about this night than that boyo. What use would he be in a battle, anyway?'

And true it was for Brian, because Dúlaing Ó hArtagáin was, unfortunately, not like other chieftains, addicted to fighting, looting and boasting. He was a very poor hand at managing a sword at all — had no more than a spectator's interest in such unprofitable work. Always he did his best to be gone, if he could, when fighting was imminent, had far and away more interest in reading old manuscripts and listening to poetry and the compositions of bards and wandering rhymers. A strange and unlikely man he was to have command of fighting-men in such dangerous times. Not that his attitude did not cause resentment! Even in the ranks of his own men there were growlings, dark and underground mutterings: 'The Devil blast it, he'll shame us. Sure, he isn't a right man, at all. In the last six months he didn't even make one widow.'

'Oh, you have the truth of it said there. He isn't worth a bag o' salt, that's what I think!'

'We'll take a vote an' get rid of him, will we?'

But this was as far as ever they got in deposing their chief, for he was reputed to have knowledge of deep spells and magic, and no one wished to be the first to test him. So they grumbled on, ritually, and Dúlaing went about his untaxing duties, as always.

However, to have to deal only with his own men was all very fine; a person might survive that. But when the son of the High King summoned in the king's name — that was a different story altogether. That was exactly what Murrough did too.

'My father is too soft entirely,' he muttered. ''Tis no wonder the country is gone to the dogs. But wait till I'm the king an' there'll be changes.'

He called a servant and sent him post-haste to Dúlaing's house, with orders not to come back without the missing man.

But of Dúlaing there was no trace at home.

'Oh, he's not here,' said his wife. 'He's gone across the mountain to Broadford to some oul' bard, listening to a new poem, I think it is.'

Off went the messenger, out over Sliabh na gCailleach, and after many enquiries and hard searching he found his man in a *síbín*, singing ballads and playing the harp, truly a man among his people, while a *meitheal* of admirers pressed in around him.

'Ohhh! For shame, Dúlaing Ó hArtagáin. For shame!' he cried, his shadow darkening the floor. 'Every other man in the land gone to fight the Northmen an' you skulking here in this dark sty. For shame!'

Dúlaing half turned, squinted at this unwelcome interrupter. 'Yerra, for shame yourself. Who are you, an' what d'you want?'

The messenger, in few words, explained, distaste etched in every wrinkle of his brow. Dúlaing listened, and a look of weariness spread over his face.

'Look, poor man, don't you know that this music'll still be played when there won't be a Dane in it?'

'I know nothing about that, sir. I was sent to get you, that's all.'

'Ah, what good is it talking? Go on. Tell the king I'll be right behind you.'

He excused himself from his audience then, with much regret, and started on the road back. And who could blame him if there was no haste in his stride, no spring in his step? Called to battle, maybe to die; that was a poor ending to a *seisiún* that had been gathering pace with every song sung, every tune played.

Meanwhile, at Kincora the news was grim. The Northmen were on the march and Brian's presence was urgently needed in Leinster if his fickle and wavering allies in that kingdom were to be retained.

'If we wait another day it'll be the finish of us all,' he said to Murrough. 'We have too much time lost already waiting for that fellow, Ó hArtagáin. He can follow us on when he gets here.'

And so they set out on the long march towards Dublin and the enemy, a journey that would change the fate of Ireland.

Dúlaing, at the same time, and all unknown to himself, was about to meet his own destiny. Slinking along Gleann na gCailleach at his slowest possible pace, and just opposite Craglea, he noticed an object lying on the path, dead ahead. He hesitated, but only an instant, for it was certainly the form of a person, though covered over with a cloak. The thought occurred to him that it might be the messenger, waylaid and maybe injured or worse. He dashed to the prone figure, pulled the cloak aside — and was at once grasped by a skinny but vice-like claw. He sprang back as if burned, but struggle as he might there was no escape. And worse, he found himself riveted by two dark eyes, glittering out of a wasted face, barely recognisable as that of a woman. Fright welled up in him, and a scream, but no sound came, only a hoarse rattle.

'Dúlaing Ó hArtagáin,' she whispered, and her eyes never wavered, never blinked, 'you're well met here this day. Late as always, you are, but a lucky thing for you that that is so.'

'I'll take your word for it, ma'am,' he stuttered, his scattered wits beginning to collect themselves. 'But who are you, an' what do you want of me?'

'I am Aoibheall' — when he heard that name he fell to his knees — 'and I have a message that you must deliver before the fall of night.'

'Of course! Anything you ask! I'd be honoured.'

'Be silent! Listen! Find Brian of the Dál gCais. Tell him that the battle to come will bring more sorrow to his land than ever a battle did. Tell him to prepare himself, for he and Murrough and three score of the chiefs of Ireland will fall. But woe betide the wearers of the shirts of iron. And woe too to Bruadair the dark-haired. For the northern skies will echo to the cries of widows after that day's work. There's many a

man even now going merrily to his death, laughing and joking as if he were to live forever.'

'How can all this be known to you?' breathed Dúlaing. He felt compelled to interrupt her, for his flesh was beginning to creep. Still her eyes held him, more securely now than her bony hand.

'Because I am Aoibheall! Oh, I listened to their chatter and their songs last night at Kincora. Even from Craglea I heard them. And I wept! For Brian, for them and for you I wept, Dúlaing Ó hArtagáin.' Her voice tailed off, and under her otherworldly stare he could feel his neck-hair rising. But there was nothing he could do, only wait for the worst, which he was now certain must come.

'Of a certainty you will be among the number of the doomed, unless ...'

'Unless?' he gasped.

'Unless you do my exact bidding. Take my message to King Brian, but for yourself take this' — and rummaging

among her garments she drew out what looked like a petticoat, but infinitely tattered and unclean, as if generations of
rats had been sucking and gnawing at it.

'Put it on you, an' while you're wearing it no harm will
touch you.'

He was between being disgusted and relieved. 'Thank
you, an' thank you again. I won't forget to do everything
you ask' — and he bowed himself away from her, a changed
man. He could hardly put his feet quickly enough in front of
each other now, and never once did he look back. He
stopped at home only long enough to demand his weapons
and saddle his horse; then he was gone, leaving his wife to
mouth her protests and questions to the empty air.

He had no notion how far the army might be gone, so he
made no delay, only spurred his mount without mercy. And
at last, near Muine Gall, he overtook the baggage-train, then
the main force a few miles on. He urged his exhausted
animal past the files of good-humoured, curious men, until
he was pushing his way towards the litter where the aged
king lay. But before he could reach Brian he found his path
barred by Murrough. There was no welcome in the young
man's mouth, only the scathing word.

'So, the brave man came at last, did he?'

Dúlaing felt the sneer as keenly as any chief might, but
there was too much on his mind to waste time trading
insults.

'Don't mind that now, Murrough. I have an important
message for your father, so let me through, like a good man.'
Something odd in his manner, an urgency that was wholly
out of character for him, prompted Murrough to interfere no
further, and so he came to where Brian sat, and told him his
news. If Brian was surprised to see him he did not show it,
showed no emotion at all, in fact, even when the chilling tale
was done.

'Well I know that you bring the truth, Dúlaing Ó
hArtagáin.'

His voice was distant, subdued. 'I was expecting it. I

heard her cry last night on Craglea mountain. But ...' — and he looked away — 'no man can live forever, and only a fool tries to run from that which is laid out for him.'

He called Murrough to him. 'Tell the men nothing. We march on, to death or glory.'

Then, as Murrough's broad shoulders swung away, he repeated, more softly, 'Death *and* glory'. And repeated it again and again, like a litany, his eyes far, far away.

Dúlaing did not see the old man after that, for as the army advanced, swelling as it went, there were other matters to divert his mind and energies, not least being whether he should wear the gruesome rag or not. The nearer they drew to Dublin the more urgent became his dilemma: was it a trick — in which case he was sure to die anyway — or the genuine article, which, if he ignored it, would almost as certainly mean his death?

His ditherings came to an abrupt end a day later, on Good Friday, 1014, at the Bull's Meadow, *Cluain Tarbh*, barely two miles from Dublin. The Danes, seeing the size of Brian's army, had withdrawn from their positions south and west of the town and were now in prepared battle stations here, awaiting whatever offer might come from the High King. For it had happened previously that they had been bought off at the last minute, and they were confident that the same would happen again.

However, there was no offer, only a brief ultimatum: submit or die. This time Brian was in deadly earnest. With Aoibheall's words before him, he was determined to rid his land of this recurring scourge once and for all, though he well knew what the cost must be. And so battle was joined. And Dúlaing, though as frightened and elated as the rest, had at least enough wit left to decide on the side of safety:

'Begor, I better take her advice an' wear th' oul' shift, for fear o' danger.'

In the bustle and crush of men awaiting their orders, he furtively pulled it on, concealed it as best he could beneath his equipment and waited for the advance to be sounded.

At length, his turn came and he was pressed forward, the battle-cry of Dál gCais only half-hearted on his lips. But miracle of miracles! He began to mow down all before him, left, right and centre. And even more remarkable, he never got a single scratch. His own men, and those who knew his poor reputation as a swordsman, were astonished but they were in no position to comment for the fighting was bitter and every man's wits were concentrated fully on staying alive. But even out of the corners of their eyes they could see that Dúlaing was clearing a veritable roadway through the Danish ranks, all without the slightest injury to himself. Something was not as it should be, and they knew it, but they put it down to his knowledge of spells and were thankful that he was on their side.

Far out in the evening there was a lull in the killing, and those of his friends and acquaintances who were still alive crowded around him, congratulating him on his outstanding butchery:

'Begor, Dúlaing, you had us fooled all down the years. Why didn't you tell us you were so handy with the *claíomh*?'

'Wasn't it a lucky thing for us that we did nothing more than talk about getting rid o' you?'

But when he saw how they limped and dragged themselves along, bloody, torn, yet happy merely to be alive, he grew so ashamed of his own pristine state that he let slip his secret. They were dumbfounded. The smiles faded from their faces.

'Ah, blast it,' said one man, 'I dunno is that fair at all to the poor Danes.'

'You're no man, Dúlaing,' growled another, 'to be fighting with a petticoat on you. What'll the women at home say when they find out? Next thing, they'll be wanting to fight our wars for us while we're at home washing the pots. This kind o' thing'll come to no good. Be sure o' that!'

Some nodded their approval of these sage words. Those more friendly to their chief merely bowed their heads, embarrassed.

Dúlaing blushed, then tore off Aoibheall's gift and swept it aside. Without another word or a backward thought, he flung himself again at the enemy, but a few minutes later he was killed — a low tackle by a little wart of a Dane cut the two legs neatly from under him.

Thus ended his promising career among the fighting men of Ireland. But it was always thus with Irishmen. Never, since the start of the world, has one of them taken a woman's sensible advice when there was foolish counsel available from his male friends. The price to pay for such folly has often been high — as Dúlaing Ó hArtagáin realised too late, his agonised eyes watching his severed legs taking their last faltering steps away from him.

The rest of the that terrible day's events — the slaying of Brian, the reddening of the water of Dublin Bay with blood — need no retelling here. They would read too much like a history-book account. Let it be said only that Aoibheall's voice, crying on Craglea that night, told the women of Dál gCais all they needed to know of the outcome of the battle long before any human messenger brought the news. And there are those, especially among the O'Brien descendants of Brian Boru, who claim that she cries there still, with a sorrow that will never abate, her memory of that terrible Good Friday of 1014 as fresh as the waters of the Shannon that flow everlastingly across the plain below.

2

MÁIRE RUA

If it took a strong and ruthless man to hold on to his land in
Ireland during the days of Cromwell, the woman who
hoped to do so needed to be twice as tough, and cunning as
a snake. Women who aspired to independence had few
friends in those times. Even the formidable Elizabeth of
England discovered this fact — though she lived long
enough to profit from the knowledge.

One of the very few Irish women to negotiate that
particular knife-edge was Red Mary McMahon, or Máire
Rua, as she is better remembered today. A fine-looking
woman she was, by all accounts, with her pale complexion
and long red hair. Little wonder that as soon as she came of
marriageable age there was a line of suitors to her parents'
door in Clonderlaw. But, though she respected her parents'
judgment she made her own choice, a man of the Neylons.
And they were no poor family, either. She always had a clear
eye for what might take her up in the world.

They were married only a short time, however, when he
died, poor man. Who knows the reason! Rumours were that
the family was delicate, but nothing survives that might
prove the truth of this in Daniel Neylon's case. Máire had no
intention of remaining single for long. Married she had
prospects, single none, so she contrived a match with Conor
O'Brien, the heir to Leamaneagh castle. Although the
marriage was happy and lasted long enough to produce five
children and see the castle extended into a noble and
comfortable mansion, Conor chose the losing side in the
Confederate Wars of the 1640s — and worse, continued his
error into the 1650s, the era of Cromwell's rule in Ireland.
Out he went in July of 1651 to do battle, but at Inchicronan

he fought his last fight. He was wounded most horribly there and brought home to Leamaneagh, more dead than alive. Máire Rua had been busy in his absence. The house was barricaded and ready for action when Conor's men arrived at the outer gate carrying their grim burden. Looking down from the high wall, she saw her husband stretched.

'We need no dead men here!' she barked.

'He isn't dead yet, madam — but he will be if ye don't let us in, an' quick!'

Whatever else may be said of her, she still had regard for the suffering; the harsh blows of life had not yet quenched that part of her better nature. She opened the gates, had him brought in, tended him herself. Nevertheless, in spite of all that she or her doctors could do, he died that night. It was a moment of mixed emotions for the young widow, for though she had lost another man she was at last her own mistress, with wealth, property and a title to call her own.

But for how long? If Cromwell's generals, Ireton and Ludlow, had anything to do with it she would soon be out on the road, begging, as was their intention for all Irish landowners, sooner or later. That much she knew very well. Of no help whatsoever were her two sons, Tadhg and Donough. They swore to take vengeance for Conor's killing, and when, shortly afterwards, they captured a scouting-party of parliamentary troops, they hanged them publicly for all to see, though she advised a more private settling of scores. She berated them for their lunatic — though under-standable — act, then retired to her private quarters to con-sider what it were best to do. It was not in her nature to wait passively for destruction to fall on herself and her family. But fall it must, and speedily, unless she could somehow ward it off. That much she was determined to do if it were within her power.

Her conclusion was that she must tackle the enemy in his own den, where he would be least on guard. Accord-ingly, early the following morning she dressed herself in her gown of turquoise and white, had her stallion tackled with the richest harness available and set off, her servants by her side, for Limerick, to meet the powers-that-be — none other than General Ireton himself, who was that very day inspecting the town's garrison.

It was evening when she and her party arrived at Limerick. In the thickening gloom they made their way through the untidy streets, avoiding the knots of soldiers lounging here and there, for a rough-looking crew they were, and their officers not a whit better-seeming. In fact, only Máire's finery — obviously that of a woman of quality and means — and her imperious air carried them safely through to Ireton's headquarters. There, at last, they were brought to a halt, and unceremoniously too, by one of the many guards on duty.

'Ho! What goes there?'

She did not answer the insulting question, only parried it with another: 'Where is the general? I must speak with General Ireton. And now!'

An officer strode forward, a hard-looking nail. He stared up at her, not in the least overawed by either her manner or her commanding height. He rapped out a clatter of questions: 'Who are you, woman? What do you here, and what rabble is this about you?'

If she was taken aback she did not show it. Looking through him, her eyes on the door, she said deliberately, 'Fellow, bring me to where the general is. At once!'

Those standing by cringed. They thought that he would sweep her from the saddle forthwith. And for a moment it seemed that he might. His arm whipped up, fist clenched, but instead of striking he shot out a warning forefinger and hissed, 'Begone! Whoever you are, go now or suffer the consequences.'

But this woman, who was seeing the terrifying spectre of confiscation staring her in the face, was hardly likely to allow herself to be bullied by a stranger of such obviously low breeding, one moreover, whose uniform and politics she despised. She chuckled. Then laughed. It was a throaty, lazy sound, one calculated to provoke. And it did precisely that. He shouted to the soldiers about him, 'Arrest her, all of them! By Hell's smoke, I will make an example of you, woman.'

'I demand to see your commander,' cried Máire. 'Deny me this, sir, and I will see you hang!'

Her words inflamed him only more. 'Hang, is it, you Irish —'

God alone knows what he might have done had not the door been flung open at that moment. Out stepped one who was obviously a gentleman. So much was clear to Máire at first glance, from his intelligent face, his sober yet decorous attire. If he seemed too young-looking to be of importance, this impression was immediately scotched by the reactions of the guards. They froze to attention, the truculent one also.

'What devil's noise is this? May not we enjoy peaceful conversation in our own house? You, captain! Speak! Whence comes this commotion?'

And then he noticed Máire, still sitting on her stallion defiantly. Of a sudden the captain was forgotten, his stumbling efforts at explanation waved impatiently aside. Slowly Ireton approached her, his countenance that of a man smitten.

'Lady,' said he, 'your hand,' and he reached her down, staring at her all the while. Máire complied with dignity. All depended on the next few minutes, her estate, her children's future, her own well-being. Even she trembled a little at the prospect.

He led her inside his quarters, three of her servants following, while in the yard his men glanced knowingly from one to the other and the spurned captain scowled. She was introduced anonymously and formally to those within, but then Ireton, taking on a more sombre aspect, sat at what was evidently his seat, stared at her standing in the floor-way and asked her in a toneless, judicial voice, 'Who are you? What is your business here?'

A lesser person, or one on more trivial business, would

have been intimidated by this sudden change of manner. But Máire, as she stood there, the object of scrutiny by strangers in an alien town, had too much to lose if her nerve failed. She knew that. So there was no bowing and scraping by her before him. She looked him directly in the eye, told him to his face who she was, what she wanted.

'I was the wife of Conor O'Brien but am now his widow.' Ireton stared. Such an answer begged several questions, all of them important. He chose a diplomatic line of approach: 'Supposing him, our enemy, to be dead, what is your purpose here? A rebel's wife you are by your own admission, but why here?'

Her answer was, as usual, direct: 'Only confirm to me my lands in safety, look lightly on the youthful deeds of my sons and I will marry any man among your officers in token of my confidence in your authority.'

Her servants trembled at her effrontery, expecting the worst. 'She'll have us all thrown into jail — if that'll be the end of it,' was in every one of their minds.

Nothing of the sort happened. Ireton, in fact, smiled. He was taken by her and by the simple way she put her case. It was some comfort to find that even in such an accursed land, among such deceitful people, the Lord had seen fit to send a straight-talking woman his way. Alas for his righteous innocence! He was yet but a novice in the ways of Ireland.

He summoned a servant, issued brief orders, and within ten minutes half a dozen of his officers were lined up along the wall, between young and old, handsome and ugly. Uncomfortable-looking they were, too, glancing uncertainly about them, like men caught in some wrongdoing. But nobody had troubled to tell them why they were summoned. Their confidence was not heightened when they, who had scrutinised so many captive enemies in their time, now found themselves inspected, and closely too, by a woman. Indignity or not, though, they had little choice but to endure it, for Ireton's eye was on them no less sharply than that of Máire.

Three times she walked that line, her alert eyes raking them, seeking to judge which one she would most likely be able to dominate. She stopped at last before a hulking fellow, shaggy of eyebrow and hairy of hand. He was no picture, by any stretch of the imagination, but big — and strong enough to break her in two, if it came to that.

'This is the man for me,' she beamed, her mind obviously made up. Ireton was surprised. His face betrayed as much. He had credited her with more discernment. But he asked no questions. If such was her choice it was no concern of his. She it was who would have to live with the consequences. Nor did Máire explain. Enough for her to follow her mother's advice: 'Beware of small men as of small dogs; long of memory and sharp of tooth are both.'

They were married there in Limerick, with few preliminaries but with witnesses in plenty, and as they rode off towards Leamaneagh the following day, many a man in that army cast envious eyes after their erstwhile shaggy companion and thought ruefully of the easeful times he would have from then on, a freshly-made-up gentleman with no more worries — financial worries, anyway.

Unfortunately for some, the promise of good times is no more than a desirable shadow, a fact that Máire's new husband quickly and horribly discovered, though the discovery did him little good. He had scarcely settled into his new home at Leamaneagh, had hardly left his imprint in the bed, when he suffered an unfortunate accident. His hand slipped while he was shaving — and common knowledge it is how treacherously sharp those old open razors were, and how dangerous! By the time the bleeding could be staunched the poor man was beyond all human help, and Máire was widowed yet again. She was disconsolate, even heartbroken, but what was to be done other than clean up the mess, bury him decently and dress herself once more in turquoise and white?

She arrived the same day at Ireton's quarters, all sorrow, of course, and that hardy gentleman was not a little surprised to see her back so soon. But he was full of sympathy for her sad loss and readily agreed when she requested that he send for more of his officers. Again she made her choice, this time a fellow of unpromising aspect, and once more she was speedily married. Ireton himself saw them off at Thomondgate, and as they turned to depart he laid a hand on Máire Rua's arm and smiled. 'Try, if you could, to be more careful this time, madam,' said he. She could not be sure whether there was a hint of warning in his voice, so much did the chatter and good wishes of the bystanders dull all subtlety. But no doubt she turned it over carefully in her mind as they made their way back to Leamaneagh.

This second 'Limerick husband' was a strange fellow. His first act, on arriving at the castle, was to leap from his horse and dash headlong for the circular staircase. The servants, who had been marshalled in the courtyard to receive their new master with every outward sign of acceptance, were amused. Well they knew what it was like to be short taken; one of them hurried after to show him the way to the garderobe. But there was no sign of him there, only the fading clatter of his boots further on up the stone steps. Moments later, to the surprise of those below, he appeared on the battlements, oblivious of their presence, only staring out over the lands that were newly his.

Máire did not even attempt to join him on his lofty perch. Too well she understood the thoughts that must be coursing through his head. After all, had she not done what she had to preserve those same lands? When he had not come down by supper-time, however, she decided to investigate personally. She climbed the eighty-nine steps and paused, slightly winded, before stepping out into the chill evening breeze. She was taken aback to hear a mutter of conversation. Who, she wondered, could be there besides her newly-beloved? She laid a finger to the door, pushed it ajar, and peeped into the fading light. There was no one, only himself, muttering over and over, 'All mine. I'm rich! I'm rich!'

She thought it better not to butt in on such fantasies, and so returned to the great hall alone and pensive.

If she expected an improvement in the days that followed she was to be disappointed, for he became if anything even more unsociable, making not the slightest pretence at affection towards Máire or civility to the servants. Morning, noon and night found him walking the battlements, gazing fixedly out on all his easily-won property, north, south, east and west.

Certainly the man was fixated, and to a dangerous degree; that could not be doubted. But whether his ailment went further — to dizziness or the falling fits — no one knows. All that has definitely survived the decay of the centuries is that one morning, in his eagerness, he leaned out too far towards the north, lost his balance and tumbled down the seventy feet to the ground. He never moved again in this world; in fact the servants had to scrape him off the bare Burren rock at the foot of the wall, a wholly disagreeable task to people of refinement and delicate digestion. But it was the least they could do for their master, notwithstanding the fact that he had been less than a fatherly figure to them.

The pity of the whole tragic affair was that there was no witness! Máire was distracted, naturally — and shed tears enough to prove it, but how could she be held responsible if he had a bad head for heights or a poor sense of balance? She consoled herself and those closest to her with the sober observation that such deficiencies, though regrettable, were to be expected in the rootless and wandering Gall. It was as tragically simple as that.

Back she went to Ireton once more, indignation creasing every feature of her handsome face.

'Oh, no,' said he when news of their approach was brought to him. 'Surely she's not here again!'

She was. And shortly afterwards she stormed into his presence in spite of the best efforts of the guards.

'What is it this time, woman?' he enquired wearily.

She attacked him then, abused him to the highest heaven: 'I wonder, sir, that you should greet me with such a question! Why cannot you give me a proper man? Shame on you, to slight me thus. These ... creatures I accepted up to now — to do you a favour, may I add — were red useless! Little chance have you of conquering Ireland if they are the type of men commanding your army!'

He made no reply to that. Maybe the poor man realised that she spoke true. For the sake of peace, he assembled another line-out, and again she made her choice, a man of lowly rank, one Cornet Cooper of the Limerick garrison. But Ireton was determined to salvage at least some of his authority. He warned her: 'This is the last one, mind. Return no more, or I won't have an officer left.'

Ever so slightly she smiled. Some such thought was evidently in her mind, too. The happy couple were married, as married as she had been before, and off they went north-westward, into the green unknown.

Now, this man Cooper was not at all content to confine himself to Leamaneagh or view his lands from the top of the castle. He was an expert horseman and determined to see every inch of his new estate for himself. Off he would go

every morning, riding here, riding there, examining everything in depth, until at last Máire said to Donough, her son,
'We can't have this. Next thing, he'll be getting too fond o'
the place entirely.' And as usual she did not lack a plan to
put a stop to his gallop!

Behind the castle was a large stable, a solid stone building, and in that stable were Máire Rua's pride and joy, two
white stallions, trained by her own hands, fed by her, and
amenable to no authority but hers.

'You can take one o' them tomorrow,' she told her husband pleasantly a week after his arrival, 'an' we'll visit our
lands up near the Cliffs o' Moher.'

Though he had no idea where Moher was he was delighted, and even more so the following day as they galloped, with the wind in their faces, north-westward towards the
sea. Little he knew that he was about to get a finger-tip view
of those majestic creatures, the Cliffs. Yet he did, for as he
rode cautiously along the edge of the awesome precipice,
astonished at the wondrous view, the heart-shaking height,
Máire Rua whistled. At once his horse reared up and only
the razor-sharp reactions of the rider saved him from instant
and awful death. He was thrown, landed awkwardly and
rolled to avoid the slicing black hooves. Unfortunately for
him he rolled to the west, a few fatal feet, and with a wild
shriek tumbled over the edge and out of sight. How
exquisitely Máire had trained her beast!

She, for her part, had no stomach for heights, so she did
not venture too close to the edge. But she waited a decent
interval. However, when John Cooper did not appear, and
showed no signs of doing so any more, she turned away
sadly and with a sigh of regret made her way slowly back to
Leamaneagh.

'How soon passes the glory of the world,' she comment-
ed sombrely to her chambermaid as she was made ready to
retire that night. Such was John Cooper's epitaph.

Máire Rua was a free woman once more, and it was this
very freedom that drew her into a wholly unlooked-for

conflict with Terence O'Loughlin, Prince of Burren, and scion of one of the oldest Gaelic families in north-west Clare. Though his family's power was now looking something shaky in face of the victories of the parliament's generals, he was still consumed by notions of his own worth, in the oldest and most hallowed Irish way. And out of his pride he looked about him and noted Máire. Thinking it a great pity that she had no man to protect such a vast and vulnerable estate, he offered to accept her if she would propose a match.

Máire was not amused. The last thing she needed was another husband. And yet ... he *was* a fine-looking specimen, strong of limb, handsome, and an excellent horseman. Who knows what the outcome of gentle persuasion might have been? But O'Loughlin knew nothing of such a subtle approach. *An modh díreach* for him, in good time-honoured fashion. He began to pester her, became the living nightmare of her every waking hour, until she could stand it no more. Unless she could shake him off she would soon be a prisoner in her own house, and that she was not prepared to endure.

So she summoned the bold Terence, welcomed him graciously enough, and after some formalities and small talk, led him to the stables and into the gloom, where he could be seen, but could not immediately see. And at once he was conscious of being watched by eyes that were at best hostile, at worst evil. He froze. But Máire spoke, and cheerfully enough: 'Now, Prince of Burren, I'll marry you if you're able to ride that animal as far as Moher — and back.' She pointed. There, staring at him, ominously still, was Máire's own stallion. And behind him stood the other, equally and unnervingly silent.

Terence did not allow himself to panic, only replied with what bravado he could summon, 'Why wouldn't I? Consider the match as made. I'll be here tomorrow to ride him out — early!'

Yet, he was glad enough to retreat unscathed for the present from that oppressive gloom in which he could feel three pairs of eyes boring through him and sense something approaching — was it amusement? — in the heavy air.

Even though Terence was very much his own man, not one much given to seeking advice or asking favours, he sought out his father that night and told him of the happenings of his day.

'What'll I do?' he concluded. 'She's out to have my life, that's sure. But I can't refuse her challenge. I'm nothing if I do.'

'You have more sense than I credited you with, *a mhic,*' replied the elder O'Loughlin, rising — with some difficulty, for the bones were beginning to trouble him. 'Leave it to me. Well I know that you have the skill to ride that stallion. But you'll never live to tell the story if you use the tackling Máire Rua gives you.' He called a servant. 'Bring in the reins an' bit that's there below under the stairs.' They were brought.

'Now,' said he to Terence, 'I'll send these on an' they'll be waiting for you a mile beyond Kilfenora. There'll be no stopping that animal once she lets him loose, so hold on for your life, an' be on the sharpest lookout for the man that'll throw these to you when you're passing. I saw her trick used before — the leaden bit an' stretching reins. Not so new, but bad enough to kill a man that was unwary. Do what I say, boy. That way, you might come back alive.'

Terence did all his father told him, though it took no little composure to preserve a calm exterior as he was ushered through the three gates of Leamaneagh court next morning. Yet, with his life at stake, determination settled on him, and so he waited for Máire to appear. Soon enough she came, and straight to the stable. She hurried to the chosen stallion, tackled him herself, all the while whispering words in his ear, then led him, blinking, into the morning light.

They eyed each other coldly, animal and man, to Máire's evident delight. It would be a battle, this one; that much was plain. But she had every confidence that O'Loughlin, for all his skill, would shortly be making his last journey.

'Mount up,' she ordered brusquely. He did as she

commanded.

A servant appeared in the doorway. She nodded to him. He in turn signalled to someone at the innermost gate-way, and immediately the lofty oaken gates began to swing shut. O'Loughlin's heightened senses took it all in, and a feeling of panic gripped him. So, it was a trap, after all. He was about to yell his defiance, and let come what might, when Máire spoke again, quietly: 'Come.'

She led mount and rider into the yard, then gestured, briefly, towards the gate that had just closed. 'Your first test, young man,' and the emphasis she put on 'young' stung him. 'Jump that, if you dare.'

He made not a moment's delay — to do so, he knew, would be fatal — only spurred the stallion, snatching the reins from Máire's clutch as he did so. The beast hurtled across the yard at a pace that shocked him, jerked him backwards. But he held on, somehow, even when the powerful hind legs catapulted them up, up and yet higher towards that terrifyingly narrow opening between the gate and the stonework of the arch overhead. Only by crushing his face into the horse's neck and holding on instinctively with both arms could he have hoped to do what he did in the next six eternal seconds. But he did it. He even survived the shock of their landing — though if he had depended on the reins alone his brains might well have decorated the cobbles of the yard. If Máire was surprised he did not see — or care — but one thing at least flashed across his understanding: why the castle had been called *Léim an Eich*, the Horse's Leap. He galloped through the two remaining gates, his courage coming stronger to him with every beat of the hooves. And no one hindered him. Perhaps it was sheer surprise, that he had done what no one had expected of him.

With a wild yelp, the cry of the O'Loughlins, tailing out behind him, he urged the mighty beast towards Moher. But if Máire was pleased that that part of her plan, at least, was going as ordained she might have been less confident had she realised what was in Terence's mind. For no longer was his concern with his own self alone. Let him but do this deed, he now knew, and his reputation would be made forever. And that of his family too.

A mile to the west of Kilfenora his father's most trusted servant was waiting as promised, at a rise of ground where he knew that even the best of horses must slow. He flung the reins and flung the bit, waved his young master a hesitant farewell and shook his head as he watched him wrestle the huge brute over the hilltop and out of sight.

'God be with you this day, *a bhuachaill*,' he muttered, 'or it'll be the hard waking for your father to bear.'

How Terence exchanged the solid bit for Máire's base article, her reins for his father's, is still the subject of conversation in the barony of Corcomroe. Many and many a one has tried to repeat the daring feat in order to win this or that petty wager, but even had any such attempt succeeded it would signify nothing. For the simple truth is that there has never since been an animal like Máire Rua's stallion in that part of Ireland. The one important fact remains: he did it, and by the time they were approaching Moher he was prepared. He had every need to be, for at the place called *Aill Briste Croí* (Heartbreak Cliff) the horse made directly for the lip of the precipice, and if Máire's tackling had been his only help, nothing could have saved Terence from a bed among the saints that night. But O'Loughlin, though he had every respect for those august ones, had no desire to join them — yet. He wrenched the reins with all his might at the last possible moment and heard the bit crunch through jawbone. The sound set his very teeth on edge.

Its effect on the horse was even more dramatic. With a scream of agony it turned over, foaming, bleeding, its hooves flailing for Terence. But he was already at a safe distance, his heart palpitating as he watched the great beast's rage.

Somehow the stallion, though it was obvious that he was badly injured, struggled back towards Leamaneagh. Terence followed close by, wondering at his strength, his great heart.

But what was done could not now be undone, and though he would not without good reason have hurt so noble an animal, he was glad that it was he who was whole and entire. For that he had his father to thank, he knew.

Half a mile from Leamaneagh, close by Máire Rua's stone chair, where she was accustomed to sit and view her lands, the stallion at last collapsed, and a trickle of dark blood from his nostril told its own story. He would never see his mistress again. Terence, in a last salute to the bravery it had shown, raised his voice to heaven for the second time that day, and unleashed the war-cry of O'Loughlin against the walls of Leamaneagh.

The response was immediate. Máire and her men were on the scene in minutes. But Terence was gone, disappeared into the very ground, it seemed, as only natives of the Burren can.

'My curse on all O'Loughlins,' she howled as she cradled her beloved beast's head, 'and on your ancient traitor father in especial' — for well she knew that Terence's skill was aided by one wiser in years than he. 'I will be revenged! Hear me! I *will* be revenged,' she screamed, then sobbed to the bareness of the watching hills about.

Thus began her vendetta against old men, aided and abetted at every turn by Donough, who quickly came to look on it as some new form of sport, akin to hunting badgers or foxes. Jointly they proclaimed an edict commanding that all those over the age of sixty be brought to the castle on a certain day. They wished to speak to these wise old ones, they said, to learn from them the secrets of so long a life as theirs. Few were fooled by this transparent device. Only those nearest the demesne responded, and that more out of fear than duty. They should have hearkened to their instincts, for when the last of them was in the castle yard the outside gate crashed shut and, too late, they found themselves face to face with a gallows. They shrank back, all, both the aged and their minders, against the gaunt walls, but it was idle for them to attempt to escape their fate. One by one they were seized, forced to climb the steps to where the rope dangled in the air, and one after the other they died, pointless victims of Máire's unforgiving rage.

The countryside was aghast at this most vicious crime; not even Cromwell's men had behaved so barbarously. Yet so long as power remained at Leamaneagh there was little to be done except to conceal all the aged ones till the insanity might pass. Hiding-places were found aplenty in caves and limestone pavements, among the boulders and at the back of God speed. But Donough, rising to the challenge, ferreted them out, a few every day, and would have made an end of all eventually had he not been halted in his tracks by a strange apparition whose power proved greater than that of mother and son combined.

He had been observing one of his Linnane tenants, a quiet inoffensive man, for some time. Well he knew that the man's parents were still alive, but so far it had suited his humour to withhold the fatal demand, and instead ..atch the poor wretch cringe in dread every time he was spoken to, even for the most trivial of reasons. But the playful mood soon enough left him and he ordered that they be handed up forthwith.

'I don't know where they are, your honour,' stuttered Linnane. 'They're gone from the house this good while back.'

Donough settled an interested gaze on him, then replied icily, 'Your life or theirs, fellow. Bring me your choice by noon.' And then, as if something amusing had occurred to him, he turned with the words, 'Bring to me your best friend and your worst enemy also. If your choice diverts me ... who knows!'

There was, however, little humour in his smile, and well Linnane knew it. The poor man was stymied. Fear in all his movements, he returned home, made his way to his parents' hideaway to break the bad news to them. But he found there a visitor, one who looked like no one he had ever seen before. With long white hair and beard, gnarled staff, tattered clothes, bare road-hardened feet, he seemed for all the world like a vision of John the Baptist. Linnane stood rooted, fear strengthening to terror in his face. Had they been discovered? Whence came this ... creature?

His father it was who motioned him to sit and listen. And thus he heard of the mysterious *Maistín Caoch na Cruaiche* and his vow to protect old people from the tyranny of Leamaneagh. Scant were the details he revealed of his own past, but his voice had the ring of some ancient authority and his words were full of comfort:

'I have been sent to aid the old, to break the bloody tyrant's hold,' he chanted, and then, more ominously,

'And from my task I may not rest till age and honour ... walk again together.' His voice quavered off oddly, and Linnane started. But the Maistín fixed him with a gimlet eye, even more unnerving than Donough's.

'Tell me, what was required of you?' that same cracked high-pitched voice demanded.

The story was quickly told.

'Your friend and your enemy, hah? Go back, and take with you your dog. No better friend have you. Take with you, too, your wife. No greater enemy have you. I will be here when you return, for I know what I know.'

The poor man was not a little perturbed by such untoward news, but as he stood uncertain what to do, his father waved him away: 'Go! You heard what he said. Do it! Every bit of it.'

He stumbled off, called his wife and dog, and set out, silent, for Leamaneagh. He still had explained nothing to the poor woman by the time they reached the forbidding outer gate, where Donough was waiting.

'So, you came, did you? But where are the cursed old wretches? Is this how you obey my commands?'

'Oh, your honour, I did what I could. At least I brought you my worst enemy an' my best friend.'

Donough noticed the woman falter, stop. He smiled, more a little grimace. It was not heeded, though, for husband and wife were looking at each other, she as if she were seeing before her a lost acquaintance met unexpectedly.

'Tell me, then, my friend,' Donough hissed, 'which is which?'

Linnane's mouth opened and closed several times before his voice at last snared the words he dreaded.

'This is my friend,' he pointed to the dog, averting his face from his wife. She stood rooted, as still as a stone.

'And who is your enemy?' persisted Donough, savouring the game. There was no escape for his unfortunate victim. Roll his eyes where he might, he was pinioned between their gazes, the one mocking, the other filling now with hate. In a last pained appeal he met Donough's eye. But he found no mercy there, only the same mocking demand: 'Tell me!'

Shaking, he raised his finger. 'She is.'

And the hand dropped limply to his side.

Donough awaited an outburst. But it was tears that came, silent tears, sobbing, and a clenching of her teeth. Still he waited. That phase would pass, he knew, then she would talk. In her shock of disbelief she would probably tell him more even than he cared to know. And so she did, her grief quickly turning to anger, and that to rage.

'I'll lead you to where the filthy oul' *bodach* is, your lordship. An' his *cailleach* of a mother, too. An' if hands are needed to tie the rope, let mine be among 'em.'

She was as good as her word, and her husband had to bear the torment of looking on as the armed servants surrounded his parents' refuge. But the person they dragged out was not Linnane. Old he was, certainly, but not the man they sought.

It was none other than the Maistín! Ragged, barefoot, his staff yet in his hand, he was hauled before Donough while Linnane gaped, lost once more for words to match his muddled thoughts. The lord, Máire herself, even the retainers, came out to behold the weird figure.

'What means this?' roared Donough. He glared at Linnane, then stabbed a finger towards the rope. 'Explain, peasant, or there your bones ...'

His outburst was drowned, smothered entirely by the cold, cracked voice of the Maistín: 'I am come,' he grated, 'to give you warning, Donough. Take heed, for the Curse of Cruach hangs on a slender thread over this place.'

It seemed to Linnane for a moment that Donough might order the Maistín's death on the spot, but it was Máire, in fact, who spoke, in a steely voice.

'Your company likes us not, old fool. Nor will we detain you longer than it takes to ready your departure.' She smiled as she said it, a wolfish grin, and beckoned an attendant to fetch a rope. The Maistín might never have heard a word. His sightless eyes continued to stare fixedly at Donough, to that young man's obvious and growing unease.

'If you but knew, O'Brien, what threats encircle you

close about' — and he raised his voice, faced now towards Máire — 'Deceit where a mother's kindliness should be, you would beg of me to tell what I know.'

'Must we stand and listen to such gibberings?' demanded Máire, bustling forward to meet the servant who had appeared, carrying a length of rough hemp.

'I for one will not,' and she snatched the rope.

The Maistín laughed to her face, and stood, daring Donough to question him further.

'Stay, mother!' ordered the lord, and in the same breath to the ancient one, 'We will hear further. You speak of threats, deceit. I would have your news, old man.'

Máire was visibly taken aback. Never before had her judgment been questioned in her own house. Nor would she stand for it! Roughly she pushed past her son, a look in her face verging on contempt. But there was yet another surprise in store for her, for Donough clamped his hand firmly on her shoulder, halting her in her tracks.

'Mother, I said stay! This matter I mean to hear.'

He motioned to the Maistín. 'Speak, sir, while you may.'

There was a pause, upon which even Máire did not dare impinge, and then the old man raised a finger that did not flinch. It pointed straight at Máire.

'Ask her why she keeps twelve young men dressed as women for her attendants. Then perhaps you will know part of what I know.'

His words could have been so many cannon, bringing destruction to those grey walls. Disaster seemed to hang suddenly in the air.

Donough turned abruptly, but the look of rage and mortification in his mother's countenance told him that here was something more than an old man's ranting. Face tight, voice strained, he barked out several orders, hardly hearing his own words. Máire's lady attendants were led into the yard and only then, waking to the scandalous possibilities of the next few moments, did he command the other servants to disperse to their duties. When they were alone he approached the fair and modest ones, but in his face was nothing of *plámás* or dalliance. Despite Máire's fieriest remonstrations he wrenched up the skirts of one after the other, and found to his horror that there was not a single woman among them, but young men all, just as the Maistín had said.

For a few moments he blinked, striving to grasp the significance of this deception. The purpose of it did not immediately dawn on him. If it had, perhaps Máire's story might have ended there and then. As it was, Donough contented himself with ordering the rope at once for all twelve 'ladies-in-waiting', Máire's violent protests notwithstanding, and when the last of those unfortunates had fallen still he turned, merely glared at his mother, but addressed the Maistín: 'Sir, you have done me some service this day. Nor will you go unrewarded. Name what it is you would have. If it is within my power, it is yours.'

'I desire only justice and safety for the old, and an end to this' — pointing to the scaffold.

Donough mused a moment, then shrugged. 'So be it.' He raised his voice then, so that the servants, wherever lurking, might hear: 'Henceforth let no old person be molested or annoyed going about his business within the bounds of my lands. I order it!'

The Maistín had achieved his purpose and he departed for his wilderness of Cruach, leaving many a relieved heart in his wake.

However, his meditations were not to remain undisturbed for long. Blood being thicker than water the falling-out between Donough and Máire did not last. Soon they were back to their old ways, first levying ruinous tolls on travellers passing through their lands and then, when all but the very poorest had ceased to go that way, closing the road entirely. It was a grievous inconvenience to the people of Burren, one they quickly brought to the attention of Terence O'Loughlin, leaving him in no doubt that they thought it his duty to do something about it.

Without so much as discussing it with his father, he made his own arrangements. Two nights later both toll-gates mysteriously caught fire, and the bleary-eyed servants who rushed from Leamaneagh to quench the flames found themselves confronted by silent, armed men with blackened faces. They were carried off, terrified, and released only in the yellowing dawn, with a warning for the castle: open the road, or worse would befall! Naturally enough, the opposite happened; tyranny rarely responds to threats. The gates were rebuilt, more sturdily than before, each with a guard-house and full-time sentry. The people of Burren were not pleased. Nor was McNamara of Tradaree, whose lands in north Clare were no longer yielding him their accustomed rent, for his collector was now receiving the brunt of Máire's anger against the world at large. Gale-days were now bringing him nothing, for all was confiscated at the toll-gates of Leamaneagh. In effect, his rent was Máire's rent, and naturally enough he was unamused. But where was redress to be found?

After many enquiries, he was directed to the Maistín and explained his case. The wise one merely nodded; he had already heard of the new exactions, and being resigned to the ways of human villainy, he was not surprised. Wearily he promised McNamara that he would intervene personally when the time was right, but for the meantime he gave him practical advice on how his money might escape Máire's clutches. The plan was so simple that the lord of Tradaree shook his head and laughed in admiration of the old man's sharp practicality. And the advice was followed to the letter on the next gale-day: a young boy, rather than the usual group of men, was sent to collect the rent due, with orders to demand a quarter of it in coppers. When his round was completed, he divided the money into three parts, the silver and gold in one purse, which he concealed, and the bulky coppers in two others. These he displayed, slung prominently over his saddle as he approached Leamaneagh. As expected he was stopped by the guards and the usual exorbitant toll demanded. He protested, of course, as he had been told to do, in order to allay suspicion. But the fat purses were there to be seen by all. Greedy hands snatched at them, but the boy pulled away.

'Keep off!' he cried. 'No grabbing, or what kind of unmannerly curs are ye, at all? If ye want money why couldn't ye be civil an' ask for it, an' I'd give it to ye.'

They stopped, and, looking at him suspiciously, asked: 'What d'you mean, "give it" to us?'

'Just that,' he replied, untying one of the purses. 'Here ye are, then,' and he scattered the coins in a wide arc from one side of the road to the other. So taken aback were they that they fell instinctively to their knees and began to scramble in the dust, fighting each other for the few miserable pence.

By the time they discovered the trick, the boy was already offering the other purse at the second toll-gate, on the same terms. And again his ruse worked perfectly. He escaped, where stronger men had failed, and McNamara rejoiced that at last a corner had been turned on the robbers of Leamaneagh. The lord of Tradaree went personally to thank the sage but the latter had already gone, staff in hand. He had judged that the time was at last ripe for a certain visit.

The first the terrible mother and son knew of his arrival was when a breathless domestic faltered into their presence, gasping out the news. They glanced at each other, rushed to the battlements, and there, sure enough, in real life, was the figment of their worst imaginings. But what was he doing? Surely ... surely not trampling and destroying their beautiful ornamental gardens!

With a curse and a shriek, Máire dashed down, all eighty-nine steps, to confront him, calling all the while on Donough for a useless *amadán* to help her destroy him once and for all. Never was that cold stairs descended so quickly, but their wrathful haste was checked by a long and ominous shadow at the door directly beneath the murder-hole.

Grimly Maistín stood, framed by the gothic light, and as their headlong dash stumbled into silence, he spoke, in a voice bereft of all emotion: 'So, my first warning was not enough! Ye force me to come again. Well,' and he clasped the door-jamb nearest him, 'since ye have chosen to persist on the road of injustice ye will have no further need of this' — his frail-looking old fingers tightening on the solid limestone block. His face fixed on them, he jerked at the stone, and to their utter amazement and horror it came away in his grip. But how could such be? Set by master masons two centuries before to last for twenty lifetimes, how could it possibly be pulled thus from its place by such a wizened reptile? Yet here it was in his hand, three hundredweight of Burren stone, as if it weighed nothing. Such things did not happen! But neither did the next, or next, for in quick succession he ripped out two more of those immutable stones.

He smiled, waiting.

Mother and son stood, still speechless, not believing what they were seeing. Then, in the silence of that narrow place, he made a move that struck horror into their hearts: he reached out both his arms to full stretch, until the heels of his palms were each pressed against a door-jamb. Very deliberately, his shoulders hunched, he began to push outward with all his might. At another time the sight might have appeared funny, even ridiculous, and the terrible duo would certainly have revelled in mocking him. But not now. They had seen too much already for that. A low groan from the intent, straining figure of the Maistín was answered by an ominous, taut cracking sound somewhere deep within the masonry. A thin trickle of mortar-dust spilled on to his shoulder, yet he seemed conscious of nothing except the task he had set himself. Máire, with a terrified glance upwards, fell to her knees. Donough did likewise, his legs weakening under the weight of fright.

'Sir! Sir!' she exclaimed, 'Do not, I beg you. No! No more, sir, for the love of God, else we are all buried.'

He did not appear to hear. She clutched at his feet, im-

plored him more urgently than before to cease, while there was yet time. 'Hear me a moment, sir! Only listen, please, and we are your good servants for ever.'

It was a most uncharacteristic, perhaps the most abject moment of Máire's life, one that even her enemies would have found difficult to credit. But faced, as she had been before, with the certainty of immediate ruin, she did what needs must: in this case begged, then grovelled.

The narrow shoulder-blades relaxed. The old thighs ceased to strain, and his breath came in a long sigh. He was not the only one who sighed in that clammy room. Máire's head dropped, Donough palmed his forehead, combed his fingers through his hair, shaking with relief.

If they imagined, however, that their troubles were over, they had much imagining yet to do, for the old cracked voice whipped mercilessly across their abject forms, and its message was brief:

'Let me be once — but once! — more disturbed by even a rumour of vile deeds of yours and I will come again. If I must, expect to see all you cherish, everything you own, laid low. I say no more. But assuredly it will be as I promise. Tempt me no further, I advise you!'

He turned, left them still quaking with fear, and vanished into the wilderness, into history. For never again was he called on, either there or elsewhere. His work was done.

His advice was mainly heeded, too, since Máire turned a new leaf — almost. No more did she or Donough interfere with travellers or accost old people going their way, but it was hardly to be expected that the ingrained habits of a life such as hers would disappear overnight. Nor did they. If she was now under severe restraint in what she might do openly, there was no one to query her behaviour at home in Leamaneagh. And there she made up for the curb placed on her public self. If cruelty had previously been only an incidental part of the daily routine of her domestics, it soon became an established code, one indeed which bordered on the inhuman. Rumours began to circulate in the country round about of servant girls hung by their hair from the corbels of the old tower for hours on end any time Máire was feeling low. Their pitiful shrieks had been heard, but faded into insignificance beside the cries of the men-servants who were hanged by their necks with fixed knots for ten minutes and more at a time from the self-same corbels so that their mistress might be kept amused and in good cheer. And what of the handsome red-haired girls who had occasionally disappeared near to the castle? Whispers assigned to them an even more gruesome end — their breasts hacked off on Máire's express orders.

'Jealous an' cranky she's getting as her looks leave her', was the local people's laconic accounting for such animality. But nothing could be proved for sure, since bodies were never found, and even if there had been proof most definite, who would have dared to confront her with it, let alone bring her to account? None but the Maistín, and since he made no appearance, all others held themselves aloof from the ugly business. And so the whispers multiplied.

Nor was it the common sort alone who were buffeted by her growing waywardness. Even the rector of Kilnaboy did not escape. She picked him to quarrel with merely because he was convenient to hand and she could not be content unless she was thwarting someone. And when he bridled, as she knew he must, and even had the temerity to advise her towards an understanding of a woman's true place, she told him in no uncertain terms where he might take his 'new half-religion' and what to do with it when he got there. He was scandalised, poor man, but she merely laughed. And when he forbade her to enter his church until she acknowledged her error and recanted it publicly, she built her own chapel at Coad to annoy him further. And it was at Coad that her young daughters, Slaney and Mary, were buried on their untimely deaths during one of those virulent bouts of plague that scourged the land from time to time in those troubled years.

'Ha! She couldn't have luck,' her enemies gloated. 'An'

'tis all right if oul' Nick don't carry herself too. 'Twould be well coming to her.'

But there was little fear of the Devil getting the better of Máire when so many more likely candidates had failed. In fact, misfortune merely seemed to steel her all the more, to emphasise the reckless streak in her. She turned to the Black Arts with a vengeance, as if only things forbidden could give her any lasting satisfaction now. And a candidate for her attentions was not far to seek.

The man most vividly recalled in the memory of Clare people of that time was Boetius Clancy, a cunning, sinister figure who had given his loyalty to old Queen Bess and held the county in an iron-fisted terror during the Armada years. Bothalam, they called him and spat at the very mention of the word. Every passing year increased the legends of his evil doings, but it was not this that attracted Máire to him. More appropriate by far, she came on him through family connection, for her younger sister, Honora, was married to his son, another Boetius, though only a pale shadow of the forceful father. Many a time she questioned him, gradually called forth a picture of the ruthless elder, who had known royal office as high sheriff in 1588. And the more she heard, the more obsessed she became with this man who, in many ways, was so like herself, and who had cheated death, if only in the minds of men. She swore that she would never rest until she had conversed with his ghost, and when Donough berated her for her folly, 'nay, lunacy, Mother. Let the dead rot in peace. They concern us not,' she answered him as if he were a small child: 'Little the young ones of today know of either this world or the next.' And she proceeded to make enquiries. By subterfuge and stealth, threats and bribes, mainly to spoiled priests and *mná feasa*, she came at last to an understanding of what must be done to bring the spirit of Clancy to account. And despite all warnings of the dangers involved, she went about what she had purposed in her usual direct fashion — but in the privacy of her reading-chamber. She was firmly determined that the squeamish

Donough would have no act or part in the adventure (as she considered it); he was told nothing, and on the night chosen for the resurrection of Clancy's ghost, the young man went to bed as usual, entirely unaware that in the highest room of the old tower-house a weird encounter was planned.

With the dim light of three candles casting shadows on the rough lime-washed walls, Máire's work commenced, but not before she had taken the precaution of sprinkling holy water in a comfortable circle around her chair, for though reckless she was not foolhardy and had a healthy respect for the dead. Then she began to chant, over and over, the secret words she had been told would summon the spectre.

What she sought came to her sooner than she might have expected, though at first she did not recognise it. She had sat a moment to get her breath and was about to replace one of the candles, which was guttering smokily to its end, when she noticed the other two flames shiver, as if a draught had caught them. Before she could investigate, all three vanished together, leaving her in absolute darkness. She blinked, to rid her eyes of the afterglow, then rose, groping for her tinder-box. She had no need of it, for already another light had become visible, one very different from any she had seen before. Beginning as an intense blue pin-prick at the window, it rapidly expanded and solidified into a shape recognisable as that of a person, though all the features were indistinct. Máire's eyes flicked towards the floor, confirming that she was still within the charmed circle.

She sat, uncertain what to do, peering with a nervous elation as the thing took on a more definite form. It was Clancy: she was sure of it, though she had never seen so much as a picture of him.

As if he had read her thoughts, he bounded towards her, stopping a mere two feet from where she sat, rigid. And she could see now that something was wrong, for though the body was indeed that of a man, the feet were misshapen, thin and cloven like those of a goat. Startled she was, but she held her place: there was, in any case, nowhere to go. But to let him speak the first word — that was what she had been warned to do, and so she would.

For a long while he stood there, an arm's reach away, glowering, his displeasure becoming more evident with every dragging minute. At last, as if under some pressing summons, he spoke, in a voice that jolted Máire, so distant did it sound from one so near.

'Is it yourself I see before me, Máire Rua?'

Here was the moment of truth, what she had striven for.

'None other, Bothalam Clancy. And I would speak with you. Grant me that and my happiness were complete.'

'Happiness? Have no truck with that. It is illusion, all. Nothing more.'

She glanced at his feet. 'What happened that you walk as might a sheep, sir? Why are your shanks become so thin?'

It was a trivial question and she knew it, but she could not resist asking, even though there were more pressing matters to enquire into. The glow that was Clancy rippled, wavered, then the hollow voice replied: 'A widow-woman's curse it was that did it. I seized her sheep — and with good law behind me — for constant trespass on my lands, and this is my reward. Beware, beware the widow's curse, Máire Rua.'

'For widows, I regard them not at all. It is you I would know about. How do you fare? What place do you inhabit now?' she asked, growing bolder as she spoke.

He became still, and paused as if considering.

'Never once did I let pass an opportunity of doing hurt. By my orders were hundreds hanged; innocent or guilty it mattered not. I cannot, nor will not, tell you where I now abide, but of this be certain: you yourself are on that same road that brought me hither, and were it not that you are here so well protected we should be company each for other. A long and lonesome way have you summoned me this night, Máire, and the return I relish not.'

The the voice became agitated, strangled even, and began to fade into a vast distance. 'Step forth,' it called, 'step forth, Máire, and comfort me. None but you may assist me now. None but ... none ... you ...'

It faded into a whisper and was gone.

Máire made no move, fearing that it might be some trick of the Evil One. She stayed within her circle until dawn had come and gone and the day was in full flight. Only then did she hurry on down, to attempt her daily round. But she did little work that day. There was too much besides to think on, matters of weight and consequence.

From that date, those about her began to notice a change in her manner, a jumpiness that was wholly new to her. Donough became so worried that he summoned physicians, but she dismissed them angrily: 'Think ye that I am come to my dotage? I need none of your physic. When that day comes, let me be fed to dogs. Begone!'

They scattered, Donough shrugged, and life — or a kind of living — went on at Leamaneagh, tense, watchful and short-fused. Máire, it was observed, rarely entered the old tower now, and never without furtive looks about and above her, as if expecting company. But, in the absence of any explanation from her, the attendants could only guess what might be wrong and attribute to her motives of their own invention.

It was a wholly unlooked-for mercy, but a mercy none-theless, that His Majesty, James II, now chose to intervene by creating a title for Donough — Baronet of Dromoland. The news lifted Máire out of her lethargy at once. They must move. She was sure of it. What further reason was there for them to remain at Leamaneagh?

'Is it to die in this godforsaken place?' she cried. 'Here is our chance to move down to where there be people. Living here has driven me half from my wits.'

Donough, not unnaturally, was taken aback. His mother ready to abandon the house that she had striven so single-mindedly to preserve! It made little sense, but the notion appealed to him for particular reasons of his own. How much better to be close to Limerick, Ennis and society, the courts, the men of influence! In Leamaneagh one might talk and talk to sheep and servants and there an end. Such a life be damned! So he made no objection to his mother's plans; rather did he facilitate her every whim.

Inside a year, work was done to make Dromoland habitable, to the innocent a remarkable feat, though in Máire's estimation no more than her due.

'Aren't we paying 'em enough, an' more than enough? Why wouldn't they have it done?'

She was never one for idle compliments, Máire.

Nevertheless though the house was complete, the grounds and ornamental gardens were still to do, and it was here that a problem arose, for on a hill-slope facing the mansion and within view of its great windows stood four *botháin*, hardly fit for animals, yet providing a modicum of shelter for three large families and an old widow. The overseer, without any hint of compunction, threw the families, young children included, out on the road; such was an everyday occurrence in that age. But in the case of the widow he hesitated when his men refused point-blank to proceed. He fumed, of course, and blustered all kinds of threats, but in his heart he knew that theirs was no groundless fear. Only a fool would risk drawing a widow's curse on himself. All of them knew stories of strong men who had done so, who had never seen another prosperous day as a result.

He decided to take no chances. Better to let Máire herself deal with it. Cap in hand, he met her as she arrived next morning, and explained the case.

'So what'll we do with her, lady?' he concluded, looking, for all the world, like a young boy confessing a misdeed. Máire had been listening intently, incredulity spreading over her face as his tale unfolded.

'What'll ye do with her? Do with her!' — that fierce voice rising dangerously. 'What d'you think I'm paying ye for, you *amadán!* Throw her out on the road, o' course, an' knock that unsightly sty. What else would ye do?' And to speed on the work, she supervised the eviction personally, sitting by unmoved while the men dragged the hapless widow from her hovel. She pleaded with Máire, implored in the name of God and His holy saints to be allowed to remain for another month, a week, even a day. She was cringing before the wrong woman; such a servile display merely irritated Máire. She pointed towards the road.

'Be going, lest worse befall you.'

Yet the widow persisted in her whinging patter, until Máire's patience snapped. In the flick of an eyelid her whip was in her hand, quivering. The widow, in a single movement, was off her knees and on her way. Máire laughed. Laughed loud and long at the ridiculous figure that the old woman cut as she scuttled off.

The poor woman, stung perhaps by misery — or pride — stopped before she had travelled even two score steps. She turned, and the terror of moments before seemed to have wholly evaporated, for most deliberately, without apparent regard for consequences, she knelt and began to mouth and mutter, spitting out the words with vehemence.

From that distance Máire could not make out their sense. But what of that? Peasants were animals that happened to walk upright, no more. And sometimes animals had to be taught who was their master. It was one of the laws of life itself. But something was wrong here. So much she gathered from the way those workmen nearest to the old woman froze, threw frightened glances from her towards Máire, then attempted frantically to hush her.

'What says she? What prayer is that?' Máire demanded of the foreman. He hurried off to investigate but was so slow of his return that she stalked forward impatiently to discover the cause for herself.

She was not pleased by what awaited her. The widow was still on her knees, but every hint of fear, of subservience, was gone. She faced her tormentor with a look approaching contempt.

'Did I not order you to remove yourself?' snarled Máire.

'Let me but offer to you my parting gift, and you will never see my face more.'

'Nor face nor gift of yours I need. Go!' and the whip cracked viciously to a snap of her wrist.

'Yet will you have it,' and her finger stabbed towards Máire. 'My prayer for you is "that pitiless Máire Rua may die with her head stretched between earth and sky".'

She said no more, for the whip lashed across her cheek, drawing blood almost instantly. A second blow, and a dozen more, followed, wherever Máire could strike her, until the widow screamed in pain. The workmen, dry-lipped, waited for the the worst to happen. Would the mistress spur her stallion and trample the huddled figure to a pulp? Or continue until she had whipped her to ribbons?

She did neither. Instead she dismounted, stood over the quivering form, jabbed the whip into it.

'Leave your snivelling, old cur,' she snapped, but then, more pleasantly, as if of a sudden she had seen a humorous side to the affair, 'perchance we will receive you better when your verse improves. Until then, arise, bard, and take your leave.'

Yet though her mouth was smiling, there was no laughter in her eyes, and to those who stood about, and grinned because there was no other option open to them, her face might well have been a death's-head. They were nauseated by it, one and all. The wretched, beaten creature limped away, and Máire once again swung into her saddle, gruffly ordering the men to be about their tasks. And many of those hard-bitten labourers crossed themselves as they returned to their work.

'She might be better off to follow that old one while she has time, an' beg forgiveness', they muttered. Retribution could not be too far off, they felt certain.

And right they were, for a few short weeks later, while Máire was leading a party of visitors from Leamaneagh to admire the new abode at Dromoland, and they were passing down by Roughaun Hill, near Kilinaboy, a fox sprang on to the road before them. As if by second nature they gave chase at once, and a hard pursuit it developed into, for this was no innocent pup, but a wily campaigner who had evidently been run before. He seemed positively to enjoy the exercise — probably because there were no hounds on his tail — and set them a stinging pace south-eastward across country towards the Fergus.

Máire was in her element, almost young again. Her companions quite forgotten, she thrust forward, intent only on the lithe brown body streaking ahead, always just out of reach. There were young active men in the party behind her, but not one of them came nearer than earshot to Máire during all that chase. She and her stallion were unmatchable, except for one odd circumstance: despite all their speed they never seemed to gain even a little on the fleeting spectre-like shape ahead. Through Corofin he led them and on by Dysert and Fountain until they reached the outskirts of Ennis. There he changed course, keeping to the west of the town, and continued relentlessly until they reached the hamlet of Clare — later to become the garrison-town of Clarecastle. Far from balking in face of the people on its crooked street, the fox loped straight through and padded across the bridge, causing many a surprised bystander to pause in wonder. Towards Carnelly he panted, Máire tirelessly behind, beginning to sense that at last she had got his measure. Towards the summit of Clare Hill he slowed noticeably, and Máire smiled; she would triumph after all, she who had never yet failed in any pursuit.

As they crested the hill she was close enough to glimpse his lolling tongue, the drag of his brush. One last effort and he was hers! A pity the others would not see her tenacity rewarded, but they were far behind now, out of her ken, mere insects crawling off the distant bridge, unsure even of where to turn next. He was hers alone! She whooped a cry of sheer animal pleasure, urged her mount to that last pinnacle of effort necessary to complete her day, and leaned forward, elated, whip at the ready. But in her moment of triumph all was brought to nothing by a simple gust of cold wind off the Fergus. Like a ghost's breath it hooked across that bare hillside, snatched at her riding-cloak and blew it forward over her head and the head of her stallion. Startled, he reared back, and Máire, her attention wholly on her quarry, was caught unbalanced and thrown upwards and back — straight into the forked bough of an oak tree. In one moment, with an undignified little crack, Máire's interest in the doings of Clare and of all this world came to an abrupt end; the conniving, manoeuvrings and plotting of fifty years all together instantly snuffed out.

When the other members of the pursuit at last came on her she was as dead as a rat. Knowing nothing of the widow's curse, they behaved entirely as they should — shocked, horror-stricken and desolate. That their ebullient and so-lively host of hours before could now be hanging in the scarecrow gait of any common felon! It was beyond belief. How could it be true? Yet, true it all too obviously was, wish or think what they might.

After their initial terrified fluster they lifted her down, covered her with her own cloak and sent for Donough. And so began the sombre sequence of events that was to end with her burial in the Franciscan Friary of Ennis on 23 June 1686, an event attended by all the chief men of the county. Friends and foes of the family rubbed shoulders there that day, all enmities laid aside for a time, at least publicly, in *omós* to the woman who had played their power-game, and beaten them as often as not, for over half a century.

However, though her body was laid securely in the earth, her spirit found little rest, if the old people are to be believed, for even yet, in the stillness of frosty nights, the thundering hooves of her mighty stallion may be heard on Roughaun Hill, galloping towards some destination forever unreachable, perhaps to the ancient oak-stump on Clare Hill, all that now remains of the tree on which she met her God. For it is there, so the old ones claim, that her ghost yet abides, fixed in the slowly-crumbling wood, never to be released until the last fragments have returned to the soil from which they first sprang untold centuries ago.

3

LADY BETTY

'Hard times breed hard people' is a saying that has been proven true time out of mind in the long and often bloody history of Ireland. It was never more true of anyone than of Lady Betty, probably the most terrifying specimen of womanhood ever to make Roscommon her home. But she was no native of that town. Rather was she driven to it by a brutal necessity and her own unlovely disposition.

A native of Kerry, she had been married young to a well-off farmer near Killarney named Micheál Sugrue, one who had enough of the substance of this world to be able to buy some leisure for himself in the form of two servant boys. Unusually for those days, but not so remarkably for Kerry, there were several books in the house, a poor library by the standards of today, perhaps, but enough to tempt the curious mind and idle hand in an age not much given to either idleness or curiosity. Nothing delighted Betty's man more on the long chill wintry nights than to read lengthy extracts from the Aeneid or the Odes of Horace to a circle of tilted, listening faces, each one intent in the firelight, savouring the ancient words even though they might understand only shards of the meaning. In that dark era of foreign misrule, the third quarter of the eighteenth century, there was respect for learning at least in Kerry. Small wonder, then, that Betty should come to look on the same books as a means of escape to ages and places far distant from her own.

While expecting her first child, she pleaded with her husband to teach her to read, and that man, intoxicated with the prospect of an heir, could refuse her nothing. And so, evening after evening, no matter how tired out after the work of the day, he settled to his new avocation of school-master to this wife who had a more than womanly inclin-ation to learn.

By the time the child was born, she had become quite a competent scholar, for she was an apt pupil. Soon there was little more her husband could teach her; she knew as much as he. There matters should have rested — learning a fair accomplishment to be savoured on special occasions. But now there was much to do about the house, what with a young child to steal away leisure-hours and the menfolk to be fed. Two more children in as many years put an end to Betty's reading-time, and ever more surely she began to be anchored to the frugally comfortable but humdrum life of a Kerry farm-wife.

Ireland of the 1750s was not a country in which security abounded, for at the whim of a landlord or his agent one might be flung into the roadway, one's furniture scattered round about, notwithstanding the screams or pleas of wife and children. However, Sugrue's landlord was that rarity among his breed: a man of rigid conscience tempered by humanity. While he lived, no tenant went in fear or trembl-ing, and because life was predictable, men worked, paid the reasonable rent and were half contented with their lot.

All that changed with the old man's death. Now there came into the property an eldest son with scant regard for Irish peasants whose names he made no effort to pronounce and whose faces he could not have distinguished even had he wanted to. In a whirl of announcements, decrees and proclamations the old secure order was swept away in a matter of weeks, and every man shivered, knowing that a cold wind was about to blow.

The first that Micheál Sugrue knew of the changed mood of the times was when his sturdy front door was assailed early one November morning by boots and riding-whip. He scrambled to open it, an unnameable fear lending speed to his bare feet. Facing him as he stood there, half-dressed, were two sullen, oafish-looking *bodachs*, each grasping a heavy blackthorn wattle, while behind them on an enormous black stallion, sat a man he had never before set eyes on. The stranger looked him up and down coldly, menacingly, and when at length he spoke, the words rattled from his mouth in a metallic clatter, like copper coins shaken from a purse. Here was no Kerryman; no, not even one of the English. He was — Micheál knew it instinctively, and trembled at the thought — a Scotsman, that new breed being imported in ever larger numbers by landlords bent on efficiency.

In a few brusque words he let it be known that he was the new agent and that from *now* all rents were being doubled. No, there would be no leave to appeal. Pay, or go. There were dozens waiting who would grasp the chance to pay three times the ridiculously low rent the too-kind old 'maister' had been content to ask. Little wonder that the new 'laird' was so ill-provided with ready cash for his pleasures in the capital.

Still threatening, he left Micheál standing dazed at the doorway. There Betty joined him moments later, for she too had been roused by the raucous voice though she had remained hidden from view.

'Micheál! Micheál!' She shook him from his stupor. 'Come in. You'll get your death.'

'Wife, we're not long for this place,' was his hushed reply.

'Shh! What are you raving about?' said she. 'Is it a *dailtín* like that to shake us, after all our time here? Don't mind him.'

But Micheál could not help but think darkly of his encounter with the new agent, and his premonitions became reality at the November gale-day when £30 was demanded of him in place of the usual £10. Indignant, he refused to pay this impossible sum, but just as quickly Murchison, the agent, knocked down the farm to one who would willingly have bid £40, regardless of his ability to come up with the ready cash. And so, in a single morning's work, Micheál Sugrue discovered that he was no prosperous farmer after all, but a man of straw. And Betty suffered her husband's indignities even more silently than he, though no less bitterly. They found a smaller, poorer farm, but Murchison, for reasons of his own, seemed to keep them in the dead centre of his sights. They had hardly broken potato-ground that spring when the rent was doubled yet again.

What were they to do? America seemed the only ray of salvation, but where was the passage-money to come from? As it happened, no passage was required. For the tide of fortune that had snatched them flowed strongly on, and from bad to worse. March of that year brought with it a blanket of frost, but also a deadly flu, grievous to those who had money to pay for physician's care, fatal to those of lesser means, or none. Sugrues' youngest child was among its early victims, and the death, together with the misfortunes that had gone before, were too much for Micheál. He seemed to lose all heart and Betty's appeals to him to think, for God's sake, of the other two and of herself went unheeded. He pined, took to the thin and miserable bed, and within a fortnight slipped quietly to meet his maker. Through her tears of misery and loss, Betty cried to Heaven for help — and heard only the echo of her own pitiful voice. She began to turn in on herself. No one would protect her and her remaining children if she could not. But such defence was pitifully weak when well-fed Murchison and his *bodachs* came hammering for the rent. A rent she could not pay. She grovelled, begged as she had never done before, pleaded for an extra week, a day. But Murchison was adamant: money in his hand at once, or out on the road. And so, with no choice left, she turned from her native Kerry, leaving behind only her widow's bitterest curse on the landlord, his agent and all belonging to them, vowing revenge if ever it should come within scope of her grasp. She walked, not knowing, hardly caring where the road might lead her. Anywhere must be better than Kerry.

However, it was not so. Through county Limerick and into Clare they struggled, but no helping hands were reached out to assist them. In such hungry times people's concern was all for themselves. Nowhere was she invited to rest her weary bones. Her second child died, sunk in the lethargy of raw starvation, near Loughrea on a cold April night, and from that time on she knew nothing of daylight or darkness, waking or sleep, until her eldest, her one surviving son, led her blindly some time in May of that year into the miry laneways of Roscommon town.

How they managed to survive is not known. Nor did anyone care. But survive they did, somehow, and stayed on, to join the daily throng of beggars infesting the straggling streets, eking out a precarious living from the scraps cast their way by the more prosperous inhabitants of the town. A poor existence it was, from hand to mouth, with no thought of any tomorrow, each day a struggle in itself. They took refuge in the ruins of an abandoned one-roomed *bothán* in one of the muddy lanes on the west side of the town, a place hardly fit for the pigs that snuffled here and there at will amidst the squalor. But it was a refuge, no matter how poor, from the terrible daily drudgery of the streets. And bit by patient bit, Pádraig, the son, rebuilt the roof and patched it — it could hardly be called thatching — with rushes. Indeed, without his help during these first painful weeks and months in the alien town, Betty would have succumbed quickly to her misery and followed her husband. Small wonder that Pádraig became her sole tenuous tie to the society of everyday humanity, a bulwark against despair and even insanity. She had no other friend or confidant but he, for neighbours she shunned, a reaction probably not unrelated to the harsh neglect on her journey from Kerry. But, strangely, what she complained of most of all was the lack of any scrap of printed word to lighten the burden of the long nights. And now her well-nigh-forgotten education began to be a burden, to heighten her resentment at the villainy of fortune. For all these reasons, as well as for his own peculiar merits, she lavished on the boy what remained of her affections, ever more so as the years passed.

For all their poverty, he grew up a quick-witted, friendly, outgoing young man, and these attributes were his greatest ally in making his way in the town. At length, he even got a job of sorts. Their cabin was distant only a few hundred yards from one of the town's two coach-inns and thither was he drawn day after day, firstly to beg from the alighting travellers, all of whom seemed rich beyond compare, but latterly to listen and observe as well. Sometimes he would be asked to tend to a horse while its master refreshed himself, and so diligently did he perform this duty that the innkeeper eventually noticed him. He was hired as a yard-boy and paid a pittance, but at least there was always the prospect of reward from satisfied customers. Laboriously he scraped together the halfpence, the farthings, until, almost a year later, he was able to buy for his mother the first gift she had ever received: a book. Old and tattered it might be, its yellowed pages blotched by must, yet it was a sign that all had not been lost to the darkness of the past. And a momentous gift it was to be, though neither of them realised it.

Betty greeted it with a kind of wonder, was almost afraid to open it. But urged by Pádraig she began to turn the pages and, as she did so, her long-denied desire to read was awakened. Aloud, she began to falter through the sentences, but soon enough it became obvious that she had lost none of her ability. Pádraig marvelled that this poor woman, his mother, should be able to do what many who called themselves gentlefolk could not. With an awakening pride he listened while she read, words from some religious sermon promising to those who suffered privation for the Lord a paradise not of this imperfect earth. Unknowing, he had bought a volume of pious tracts, but it mattered not at all. Now that he had heard the little scrawls brought to life from the frowsty pages, he determined that he too would learn to read. And it gave Betty no small satisfaction to be able to give her son at least this, since she saw herself a failure in so much else. Every night from that time on, by the feeble glimmer of a tallow rush-light, the work went forward, unsuspected either by neighbour or anyone else in that perished town. Thus did history repeat itself.

Soon Pádraig was reading of his own accord, to Betty's great delight. It rekindled in her a kind of hope that things might yet change, become better. Now he could decipher the notices which plastered the inn walls — advertisements, auction posters and the rest. He became the interpreter, for all his illiterate fellow-servants, of the dumb print; even his master consulted him on occasion, for as well as the ability to read he began also to make a fair shape at writing.

This new-found power of words, though it gave pleasure to him and to Betty, also, through him, did something else. It fired in him a discontent, a dissatisfaction with the way things were. Why, he asked his mother, should they have to live as they did, practically on charity, when he saw others no more intelligent, no more willing to work than he, who yet were rich beyond all reason? She had no answer now, any more than when Murchison had set her wandering years before. Pádraig began to draw conclusions of his own, and his first and strongest impression was that money, far from being that root of evil beloved of all comfortably-off preachers, could be the release from penury that they so longed for. But where was it to be had? Certainly not in Roscommon. Most probably not in all of Ireland. He had spoken to enough tramping fellows from the four corners of the land to know that other places were equally without prospects.

He was unsentimental enough to realise that he must emigrate, and to America. Pointless to go to England, where the poor were in worse plight even than in Ireland, herded into dark mills and gloomy manufactories to slave out their few years, before being flung aside, broken. He knew that some of his neighbours were being supported solely on what sons and daughters in America were sending home, and he decided to do no less for his mother, who had given her all for him.

But Betty would hear none of it. Lose her only comfort?

She would prefer to die — she *would* die, if he were to go. He had to put the idea to one side for the time being, but always it stayed with him, his fondest dream, his mother's worst nightmare.

At eighteen years of age, he was more determined than ever. Week after week his friends and acquaintances were leaving, all anxious to be quit of a country that required them only as slave-labour. Pádraig grew restless. He must go, he told her. Others would seize what might be his if only he were there to take it. Still she was adamant, and for the first time a coolness grew between mother and son. Outwardly he remained as dutiful as before, but no longer did he instinctively confide his every hope and fear to her.

The final break came in April 1775, a time when great events were shaking the colonies at the far side of the Atlantic. Pádraig's closest friend decided to leave, claiming that now was the time of opportunity. Miss it and they would rot forever in Ireland. Fired by his words, Pádraig attempted once more to make his mother see the case as it truly was. But she was deaf to all his pleas. What would she do without him, a poor widow defenceless against the world?

This time he was not to be dissuaded. The same night he packed his meagre possessions, joined his friend on the Dublin Road, and by dawn they were many miles from Roscommon town. At first light Betty arose, as usual, to prepare Pádraig's porridge, the only food he ever took before his day's work at the inn. She soon enough discovered his absence, and though a lurking fear nibbled at the corners of her mind, she went about her chores as usual. But in no long time it became obvious that her worst dread was to be fully realised. Gone he was. She could no longer doubt it.

Distraught, she rushed from the cabin, to this and that neighbour's door, breathless, enquiring. They were astounded. Never before had the 'Dark One', as they had long called her, saluted them, let alone visit their homes. Aloof, only half-sympathetic, they watched her frenzied dashing here and there. A crowd collected, amused by her antics, for now she was babbling to herself as she darted about, conducting an argument with someone, it seemed, someone that only she could see. Before long, some of the older boys had begun to jeer and mock, and others, seeing that their parents did nothing to prevent them, joined in. Soon the first stone was thrown and within minutes the distracted Betty was in full flight to her cabin, a hooting but mainly good-tempered mob in hot pursuit, delighted at how diverting this boring day had suddenly become.

She slammed the door, barred it, and for a time huddled in fear as rubbish, stones and lumps of horse-dung thudded against it. But gradually the cat-calls died away; parents were again reining in their young ones now that the prospect of further sport was gone. The crowd dribbled away and Betty, freed from immediate danger, began to slip down the gradual incline that speedily led to the steep cliffs of anger, bewilderment, accusation and despair. For weeks no one saw her, even though they kept the little house under the closest scrutiny. A rumour went the rounds that she had died. It was almost the truth, but not quite.

Those first hours and days without Pádraig were comparable only to the terrible time when first she came to Roscommon years before, but worse. Yet, though every instinct in her egged her on to release her grip on such a treacherous world, she could not, for there was something else in her, too: a hardness that defied even herself. She took to living like a nocturnal animal, creeping out only in the deadest hour of night to scratch out the essentials of life. The only evidence that she was still alive was the thin wisp of smoke from her chimney, and people wondered at that. What was she burning? Where did she come by the fuel? The suspicion grew that she must be enchanted, moreover that she had the power of invisibility. Who could doubt it? All the evidence needed was there. Or so went the popular reasoning. Yet no one dared interfere now, for fear of what she might be capable of inflicting. Had they had the wit to question the landlord of the inn he could have set their minds at rest — at least as regards her food. For, out of regard for Pádraig's loyal service at the premises, he determined that he would not let the mother starve, so long as it might be done discreetly.

Thus Betty scraped through a second bitter crisis, one that might have shattered a character more brittle. But she had grown sharp as bile from this, her latest shock, and each passing day increased her edge. Worse, there was no one now to notice her shrinking humanity and cry halt. Long hours she spent, cursing, in her tiny kitchen — cursing everything and everyone, from God to Pádraig to herself. Then by turns she would become lightheaded, cackling away like one insane. It was the lightness of one who has nothing more to lose.

Months passed with never a word to ease her fathomless misery and pain. She wished, many a time, that Pádraig had died with his brother on the road from Kerry. That way, at least, she would have a mother's grief as a sort of comfort. But this ... to be deserted! She tried desperately not to think of it, for she knew that it would turn her mad.

Then it happened. Over a year after his deceitful crawling away, came a message, delivered to her by stranger's hands. She snatched it, shocked at the solidity of the thing. A letter? From whom? Or where? Her learning served her curiosity well; she recognised the handwriting at the first glance. And clearer by far, even to the most ignorant eye, was the banknote that peeped from behind the broken seal, exposed by her trembling fingers. American it might be, or English, or French; she did not know, for all currencies are as one to those who are penniless. She mouthed words, but no sound came. Oh! Her cruel and thoughtless wishing of evil on the poor boy! She read his story eagerly, how he had worked for months in Liverpool, lived roughly and eaten sparingly while he scraped together his passage-money; how he had sailed at last for New York, had discovered the city in the hands of the military. Hardly had he found his feet in the new land when he was swept up, with hundreds of others, by one of His Majesty's recruiting gangs. But, having fled one land of privilege, he was damned if he would help defend that same privilege in his new-found haven. He had deserted at the first opportunity, taking his weapon, and joined first a local rebel militia, then the forces of the Continental Army in their life-or-death struggle. He had, he said, even spoken once with the great man himself, General Washington, and he hoped when next he wrote (if God spared him) to have great events to report, since it was rumoured that they would soon be engaging the forces of the crown.

Betty's hands shook. To steady them she hugged the letter to her and leaned back against the fireplace, eyes shut, her thoughts and emotions in a whirl. He was alive. Alive! Nothing else mattered. Pádraig alive! Who would have dreamt it, after this time? Truly it was a dream come true, and for some months she revelled in it, reading and re-reading each letter as it arrived. In all five came, each telling of places and events she hardly understood — Paoli, Valley Forge and God knows what. All that mattered to her was that he was safe and thinking of her.

Then came his news of Yorktown. There was something in this letter absent in all the others, a fierce joy, a pride in the new homeland that he had helped to win. It gave her pause. Did this mean that Ireland was home to him no more? That she would never see her son again? The usual banknote had accompanied this letter, but it lay on the table, unregarded. The first stab of realisation had spread its ice through her blood as she read, and try as she might she could not shake it off. She prayed, frenziedly, that he might return to her, but there it was in black and white: he was going west, into the wilderness, to claim the land that had been granted him in lieu of wages. Mercifully he made no mention of the kind of territory it was, trackless forest, inhabited by Indians, untravelled by any white man. Perhaps it was that he did not fully appreciate its dangers himself. In any case, he would write, he said, as soon as he reasonably could.

With foreboding, Betty tucked that letter away with the others, and did the only thing possible: waited. Six months passed. A year. Two years. No word came. In that time she aged noticeably, wrinkled and greyed. But these were only the visible signs of a far more subtle change. For now she argued with God, cursed him, no more. From hoping too long, she finally became convinced that her spirits had been raised only so that they might be thrown down all the more brutally, that Pádraig had been given back to her briefly for the sole purpose of tormenting her.

Four years passed, and the silence grew ever more deafening. Hope finally died in her, not with any great angry outburst, but with a falling of head and a weary glazing of the eye. And though she trudged the laneways once more, it mattered not at all, for she seemed conscious of no one's presence, only moved like a misfortune crazed with too much dreaming.

Another winter stalked in, one she was but poorly prepared for. Whatever money Pádraig had sent was long gone, though she had squeezed its value out penny by single penny. Equally hard to face, the roof was in pitiable disrepair once again now that there was no strong hand to cut the rushes to re-thatch it. She dreaded the coming of the monotonous grey rains that would find their way in through all the weak places, even those she had stuffed hopefully with rags and grass.

November came, and with it the first teeth of the dark season. A storm had been threatening all day: those who observed weather-signs predicted that it would be 'one to rise roofs and lower heads'. And they were right. Darkness arrived early that evening, and on its tail the wind, feeling its way hesitantly at first but soon rising into a growl, then a shriek. By ten o'clock no one dared stir abroad for fear of flying debris. Those who could, slept; the rest huddled by their firesides, praying that they would still have a roof over their heads come morning. Betty's case was worse than most, for to be without a companion on such a night was a fate that not even most brute beasts had to endure. Alone she listened as the rafters shivered and groaned. Alone, knuckles white on knees in the dark, she awaited the fatal cracking that would render her roofless.

About midnight, there was some slackening of the wind, and then came the inevitable rain — sheet after solid sheet of it from the raven-black sky. It hissed and pattered in the embers and within minutes the first drops had begun to poke their way through the thatch and onto the mud floor. Wretched, she watched, or rather listened, knowing that it was futile to attempt staunching it. She hoped that the scraps of sacking and boards she had rigged up over her straw bed would keep off the worst of the wet, that was all.

Perhaps it was the weariness of watching, maybe the monotonous regularity of the sooty drops falling; whatever the cause, she dozed. Then, suddenly, there came a loud clatter. She jerked into wakefulness all of a sudden, her first flustered thought for the roof. Through bleary eyes she saw it still intact, and from the dark she could hear again now the drops that had never ceased their spattering into pools on the floor. She sighed. Better to go to bed and be done with this futile vigil. But no more than two steps had she moved when the door was struck hard several times. The selfsame rattle that had woken her! She froze. Who in God's name could it be at this time of night? On such a night! What blame to her if she hesitated to open? Another bout of knocking, this time accompanied by a voice that seemed to be muffled.

'Ho there! Anyone within? Answer, for Heaven's sake!'

Finding her voice, but approaching no nearer to the door, she croaked, 'Who is it? Who are you?'

'For the honour of Christ, open up, let me in. 'Tis a pitiless night here outside.'

Something in his voice — maybe the implied prayer —

75

convinced her that this was indeed a benighted traveller. 'But why should I care? Who gave me help with my thatch, or with anything else, either?' she thought.

The voice sounded again, the face obviously pressed to the door. 'Is it so you'd have me die of cold out here? Open, and let me in, I beg you' — and then — 'You won't be the poorer for it.'

She reached for a sliver of bog-deal, blew it aflame from the fading embers, and moved quickly to the door, her mind made up. What had she to lose? Her life? Would even that be of any great consequence to anyone? She lifted the bar and immediately the door swung in against her, almost catching her off balance. Then it was that she saw her visitor, faintly lit by the guttering flame, a tall man, sallow-faced, bearded, but so sodden through that she could not bring herself to fear him. One gloved hand held something behind him while he still clutched his dark heavy coat about him with the other. The thought did spring to her that he might be concealing a weapon, but a throaty grunt from the darkness outside quickly dispelled this: it was his horse, dark as the night itself and no doubt as uncomfortable as its master.

Before she could object, he was drawing the huge animal firmly into her tiny kitchen, pulling down its head to avoid the door-lintel.

'Pardon my boldness, ma'am,' he smiled. 'I will explain. But first, let us close out this cursed weather.'

She gaped at this effrontery. A moment before begging, now he was taking over the very house — 'Sir, who are you? And what ...?'

A flick of his fingers silenced her queries. He was glancing here and there, taking in as much of his surroundings as the gloom allowed.

'A moment to compose myself. That is all,' and he tossed the reins over the horse's saddle. The animal stood, as if it understood the delicacy of the situation.

Laboriously he began to peel off his saturated gloves. Then, satisfied that his numbed fingers were still in working order, he undid his collar, shrugged himself out of his heavy topcoat and looked about him for a place to lay it. Betty, a lifetime's subservience at her back, automatically reached forward to take it. He did not resist the offer. Smiling, he brushed past her to the hearth, rubbing his hands vigorously.

'A night,' he intoned, 'not fit for a dog. And do you know,' he added almost mockingly, 'if I had believed the people of this county I would not even be here tonight. Three hours to Roscommon town, they said. Lord God, even on the king's own highway one could scarcely make that time. But on bog-tracks such as these ...!'

Who was this man? So impatient. So ... so foreign. Even his accent was no way Irish. Or English — at least not in the way she had occasionally heard those gentlemen speak who alighted at the inn. And there was something else that troubled her about him, something so obvious that she dared not ask it. Better to let him speak it himself, for surely he could not long delay in telling her why he, a gentleman, was here, in her miserable house above all others he might have chosen, even on such a night.

And so the minutes passed. But no explanation came. He merely sat, observing her closely, though quickly averting his eyes whenever she returned his gaze. The rain continued outside, and now that the fire was dead the kitchen had become cold. Still he made no move, either to explain himself or go. At last, teetering on the edge of dozing off, she forced herself to put the unspoken question.

'Pardon me asking, sir, but are you going to spend the rest o' the night in this cold kitchen?'

'I am,' he answered directly, 'if your hospitality allows, that is.'

'But sir, this is a poor place for the likes o' me, not to mind a gentleman like yourself. Late an' all as it is, there must still be comfortable places that'd take you in. The inn up the road there, now ...'

'Full,' he replied. 'But rest easy. I have put up with

worse lodgings than this in my time. Be sure of it. All I ask now is a bite to eat and a place to lay my head and I will be beholden to you for as long as I live.'

The careless way he voiced his needs brought a tenseness to Betty's throat. The rich! All the same. No notion of what it was to be without a 'mere' matter of a bed or a meal. Her voice answered him more harshly than she had intended: 'You'll get no supper in this house. What I hadn't for myself I can't give to you!'

He sat bolt upright, stared hard at her, a peculiar expression on his face. She thought that she might have said too much, that he was about to strike her. But no. He merely muttered two words — 'No food!' — in a tone of alarm. He was about to say more, but changed his mind, and instead reached for his topcoat. From an inside pocket he fished out a bulky pouch, carefully undid its draw-strings, then hesitated.

'How much do you need to feed all three of us well?' he asked softly.

She shrugged. What did he mean by 'well'? Still he paused.

'A shilling, an' we'll do well enough,' she answered hurriedly.

'I mean *eat*, woman. A shilling would scarcely see the poor animal there fed aright. Here!'

He took a gold coin from the purse. 'This should see to our needs for the moment. You know best where to procure whatever is necessary.'

Involuntarily, she bowed as she took the sovereign, gazed a moment at the fortune in her palm. Then she quietly wrapped her shawl close about her, lifted the bar and disappeared into the night, leaving her visitor awhile to his own devices.

He was visibly astonished when she returned less than forty minutes later laden down with food for them and fodder for the horse. How could a man like this know that not an inch of those lanes and streets was unknown to her, that she had crept along every one of them at all hours of night during the years of tortured sleeplessness and solitude since Pádraig had left?

She was equally surprised to find the fire once again blazing in the hearth. How had he fuelled it? Certainly not with her few pieces of furniture: dresser, table, stools were all still as she had left them.

'Where did you get the sticks, sir?'

Waving so trivial a matter aside was easy for the tall stranger, his only comment: 'The places I have been to, ma'am, often I needed a good fire in a hurry. It is no safe matter to sit too long in the dark alone.'

Whether she understood him or not, she had much to occupy her thoughts as she prepared their meal. They ate, at length, in silence, she too dazed by the night's turn of events to contribute much, he somehow sombre, as if cogitating some great intent. Still he said nothing, merely sat, back to the wall, hands clutching his waistcoat, or now and again stroking his moustache abstractedly. Finally she moved to clear the table.

It was as if a spell had been broken. He stood, suddenly decided about something, and asked her directly, 'a bed for the night, ma'am. Is such to be had? I have travelled far this day. My senses begin to wander for lack of sleep.'

Well she knew that there was only her own straw mattress beneath its piece of protective sacking. She hoped it was still dry. What might a gentleman like this think if he found it damp, or worse still, wet?

'S-sir,' she stammered, 'you had best look elsewhere. My poor house is hardly the ...'

He cut her off politely but firmly. 'Ma'am, it is elegant. I propose to travel no further afield tonight. Any space will do, I assure you.'

She saw that he was not to be dissuaded, and gestured resignedly towards the room. 'Take it. I'll do here by the fire. I have enough time spent here anyway at night, thinking to myself.'

He flashed her an odd glance from under his dark eyebrows but said no more. In any case, she was already gone, tossing the threadbare blankets into a pathetic semblance of respectability.

He retired then, pausing only to bid her goodnight. If she noticed his shamefaced look at the moment she took her seat by the hearth, she gave no indication whatever. His last glimpse of her in the gloom was of a woman of middle years, prematurely aged, hard in profile, with iron-grey hair. He turned away, head shaking, intent, it seemed, on his rest.

Betty, at the fireplace, could not rest. Oftentimes her eyes wandered to the bedroom door. Nothing. Strain as she might, her ears could detect no sound. And so she dozed. But the discomfort of her perch soon woke her. With a groan she rose, clutching her back. She began to pace the little kitchen. Inevitably she found herself by the bedroom door. She paused. Listened intently. No sound, except for his regular breathing.

With a sigh she returned to her hard seat. But sleep came to her no more. Instead, a kind of animal alertness grasped her — for of a sudden she thought of that purse from which he had so lightly drawn the gold that had opened doors to her this night, doors that had previously echoed impassively to her pleas. In that silent moment the vista of a different existence opened to her mind, as far removed from her present squalor as is light from darkness. And all ... all in that purse. If she could only see it for a moment, feel its warmth, it might bring her luck; it would surely renew her hope in life. As quickly as stealth allowed she glided to where his coat still lay, paused to listen, then thrust her hand into its dark folds, still clammy from the recent wetting. Papers in a bulky packet rustled faintly to her touch, but to these she paid no heed. For the object of her search was already in her grip. With some difficulty she tugged it out, the contents clinking softly as she did so. She cursed under her breath, clapping a hand to the yielding leather and glancing at the bedroom door. Nothing moved. She padded to her seat, turned in towards the hearth and, with fingers that never faltered or trembled, she undid the thong, all that separated her from the vision of a golden future.

The contents did not disappoint her. Comfortably the coins nestled like soft eyes unblinking in the gloom, quietly inviting. Breathlessly she stroked the pieces. At least forty of them there must be, she estimated. Forty pieces of gold! Never had she held such a fortune in her hands before, and the very idea of it staggered her. Here, in such tiny space, was enough, and more than enough, to have held Murchison and his hirelings at bay. With this collection of magic metal her husband need not have died, nor her child on the long road, and Pádraig would never have had to cross the sea. Such thoughts, as she gazed long and lost on the sovereigns at her fingertips, seemed to remove the money from the realm of the everyday, to endow it with a power that was mysterious, miraculous. With it she could leave this miserable town, live like a human being again, even journey to America and search Pádraig out. Without it a pauper's existence and a nameless grave in the workhouse field would be her fate. Opportunities like this came once in a lifetime only. Let it pass and she would regret it for the remainder of her days. Was it not Pádraig who had said some such words?

She peeped back at the room door. Already the logic of her desires was beginning to snap at the heels of her wild imaginings. She stared, her teeth clenched, knowing the solution even before her mind articulated it: he must die. What right had he, a stranger, to keep from her her dreams? In the darkness of her quivering mind a blight spread itself on the buds of humanity, especially on that delicate growth, pity. She rose, laid down the purse and deliberately took from the dresser drawer the only sharp knife she possessed.

As if in a trance, she seemed to stand by, almost detached, while her hands did the treacherous work that her mind dictated. She marvelled at how swiftly they managed it all ...

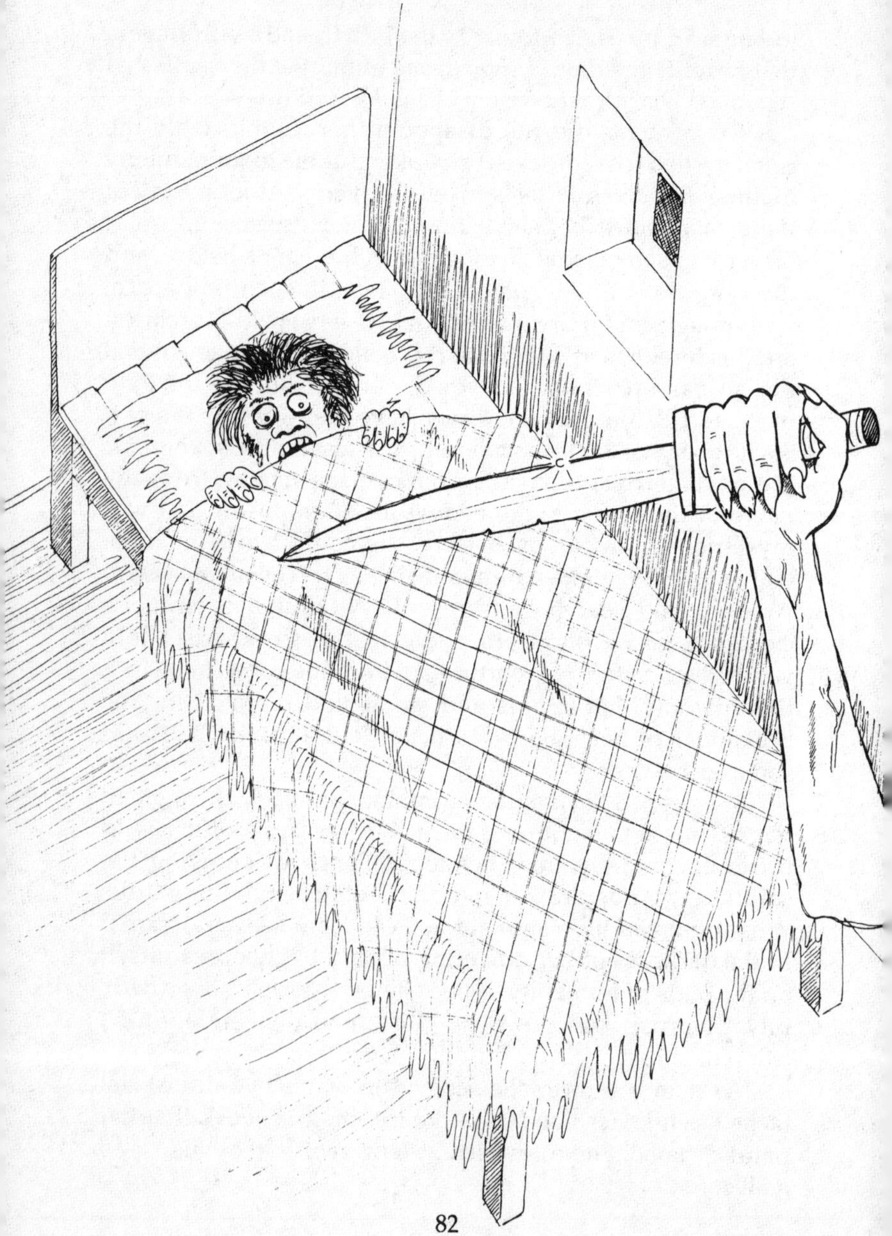

When next her thoughts gathered themselves to a semblance of reason she was once again at the hearth, along with a purse which was now hers. In her hand was still clenched the knife, blood in ugly streaks along it. Her face, set like a mask of ivory, had closed to everything that might be detected from the outside. Only when her memory focused on his sudden intaken breath, the whimper of pain as she plunged the knife into his chest, how he had struggled up, thrashed madly in his efforts to ward off her second, her third blow ... only then did the mask come to life, the fingers stir themselves. She swayed to her feet, shaking her head violently as one might to clear away a sudden spasm. Then for the first time she seemed to catch sight of the weapon she held. With a start she flung it from her and cringed, gaping, pawing the wall behind her as if expecting to be struck out of the terrible air. Perhaps she saw again her victim's face twisted in agony, his shocked eyes dimming in the miserable light with which dawn was beginning to probe that dingy room. Vainly had he tried to say something as he shuddered back on to the damp straw. He was still mouthing when his eyes closed a final time.

Listless of a sudden, she sank down beside the delightful, malevolent purse, still waiting where she had left it. And so she was rich at last! Oddly, it did not seem to excite her now. For a reason unknown, rooted too deep for her to understand, her thoughts returned always to his face, drawn by those horrified eyes. Whose son was he? What mother or wife would never greet him, kiss his bearded face again? The thought made her uneasy in herself — not for what had been done, but out of a sense of morbid curiosity. *Who was he?*

Those papers — they might give some clue. After she had read them they would make a fine blaze. Then she could think more clearly of the problem of getting rid of the body ... and the horse, of course. Nothing that a little darkness might not help her solve. It had been her friend before, and would be so again.

Her spirits began to revive. With a certain grim optimism she shook the packet of papers free of the heavy coat, brought them to the window, scattered them on the sill. Several, she noticed, were cuttings from newspapers and these she glanced over first, as the more easily readable. But what were they? Accounts of some adventurer — an Irishman, too, if she were not mistaken — who had made good here and there. But where? The places mentioned meant nothing. She was about to brush the fragments aside and examine the handwritten letters when one particular line pulled her up of a jolt. For there were the words 'Patrick Sugrue'. Several times she read the piece, but still nothing more distinct than unease registered with her. Yet, an undefined sense of urgency spurred her fingers to examine the other letters now. She had read no more than a line or two of the first page when her skin began to crawl, her heart to pound.

No! It could not be! Not! Not! She squeezed her eyes shut to blot out the grey rags of daylight and to hide what she already knew could never again be hidden. It was the self-same writing as in the letters from Pádraig, those that she had read and re-read until she knew every turn of every character. She gabbled prayers then, rocking back and forward, palms pressed to temples that were beginning to thunder to the beating of a slow infernal drum, louder, louder, ever louder. The very beating of Doom it seemed, and her throat tightened into a terrified voiceless scream as she flung herself at the door of the room where her dead son lay.

The first inkling her neighbours had of the misfortunate act was when she was seen leading the black horse from her doorway some time in the mid-morning. It was a circumstance that cause no little surprise, such a fine animal in a lane like theirs. Naturally, she was challenged, though good-humouredly.

'Who'd you do away with, Betty, to get the horse?'

She stopped dead, trembling, and when she turned towards him, her ghastly eyes told the mocker more than he

wanted to know. If ever he had seen the walking dead it was in those two eyes. He cringed back, horrified, but she pursued him grimly, step for step, her hands held stiffly, stalkily before her, clenched for murder. Half stumbling, he ran, and Betty broke into a thin mirthless cackle, which rose gradually into a scream, then a petrifying banshee wail of pain and desolation. Doors flew open all along the lane and heads appeared, alarmed faces around every jamb. Fright changed to astonishment when they saw who it was. They collected around her, gaping alternately at her and the horse. A few questioned her, in vain, and then one, more resolute than the rest, grasped her shoulders, shouted to her for God's sake to leave off her insane howling.

'You're frightening the life out o' the children, woman!'

Her lamentation trailed away into a low moan and finally a rasping gurgle.

'Tell us, what ails you, at all?'

Her head sank onto her chest, her shoulders slumped. He was about to ask the question again when, ever so slowly, stiffly, she raised her arm, her hand, towards her hovel and stood, looking down the length of it, with eyes that were empty of sight, yet filled with seeing.

Every head turned in the direction her pointing finger indicated. Utter silence settled on them all. Not a movement, not a breath. The black mouth of her doorway gaped dumbly back at them. They stood, hushed, as those stood who awaited the coming of Lazarus from his tomb. But nothing stirred, though each passing minute felt to their expectant senses longer than a day.

Finally the bold one could contain his impatience no longer.

'I won't be long finding out,' he murmured, and strode, determined, into the darkness of the kitchen. Hardly had he left their sight when he shot back out, cannoned off the doorjamb and half sprawled into the laneway, spluttering, gesticulating two ways at once.

'*A Chríost is a Mhuire Mháthair,*' he panted. 'Oh! Oh!

Inside ...'

They were dumbfounded. What in the name of God had he discovered? He was already back on his feet, backing away from Betty, his face filled with horror and loathing.

'We should have killed you that first time,' he hissed. 'Killed you, you witch.' His voice rose, close to hysteria. 'Witch! Filthy, murdering witch!'

Unhearing, uncaring, Betty turned, her face dead. She began to walk, without regard, it seemed, as to which direction. The crowd shrank back, let her pass, still too startled to hinder.

Events thereafter moved quickly to their conclusion. Others plucked up courage, supported each other into the gloom ... the body ... gold ... darkening blood ... the rush of feet as the soldiers passed in hot pursuit.

They found her without difficulty, plodding northwards on the Tulsk road, though it was doubtful whether she knew that such a place even existed. She did not resist arrest, even when they handled her roughly; in fact, she hardly acknowledged their presence.

She was lodged in the gaunt old jail, last rooming-house in this world for many a moonlighter, sheep-stealer, footpad and Ribbonman. In its cramped and verminous confines she was left severely alone, for her features, long grown forbidding through poverty and solitude, had now taken on a rodent malevolence that spelled danger to any who ventured near.

Eventually the Sessions came round, and the jail, now packed to its capacity, was speedily to be cleared. Betty's death sentence was a foregone conclusion, but she did not want for companions on her journey to the gallows the following morning. It was, after all, an age of crude violence and equally crude justice. The crime committed was the thing; motivation was considered not at all. Therefore, she, who had so brutally taken a life, was accompanied on her last journey by twenty-five others, most of whose crimes were in no way as great as hers. Pickpockets and cattlemaimers they were, fairground cheats and counterfeiters, but they all trudged now in the same jingling chains, all faced in the same direction: towards the scaffold.

As they emerged in pairs from the jail gate they were pressed upon by a noisy mob. Some, it was clear, were friends and relatives of the condemned; their cries and tears were eloquent testimony of that. Most, though, had come merely to gape and be entertained. Only with many curses and much punching did the soldiers clear a path for the doomed ones. Even this became impossible when Betty appeared. A loud groan and a scatter of hisses greeted her, but she returned them only a look of haughtiness, of contempt, even. It was this that drove the bystanders to a kind of frenzy. Threats and curses were shouted, fists shaken; soon a stone was thrown, and there would have been a mob execution and a riot had not the commanding officer fired his pistol in the air and ordered his men to make ready for action.

A crisis was averted for the moment, but the proceedings were speeded up now for fear of any recurrence. The first pair were hauled on to the scaffold, the ropes prepared to receive their burdens. The sheriff sat impassively by on his splendidly got-up grey, surrounded by a flurry of his officials. Silence settled on the people, except for a few stifled sobs.

But where was the hangman? A sudden buzz of conversation in the crowd, a restless swaying, began to unnerve the commanding officer. He jostled his way to the sheriff's side, muttered, fingered the air impatiently. The sheriff nodded sharply to one of his underlings, who scurried back through the jail gate. When he scuttled back moments later it was obvious that something was very wrong.

Terrible news! The hangman had been taken ill, he reported. There would be no hangings today. The notion quickly conveyed itself to the crowd that the sheriff was in a predicament. But to that worthy, matters appeared in a much simpler light: the executions must take place. Any other course was unthinkable. But who now was to perform the unsavoury task? Certainly not he. A man of refinement, sensibility, soil his hands with blood-soaked hemp! The idea was preposterous. And strange to say, not one of his minions was anxious to do so either, though among *them* were no gentlemen. Nor would the officer volunteer his services, or command his men to do so.

The prisoners were not slow to sense that something was amiss. The embers of hope began to flicker again in their eyes, for it seemed that a merciful providence had intervened to reprieve them.

They were to be sadly disillusioned. When the silence was at its deepest, expectation at its most tense, a voice rasped the air. 'My lord! My lord sheriff!'

It was Betty. She had spied a fingerhold on life for herself. Anxious to get to it first — for she knew that it would support only one — she gabbled out her words, but in that teetering silence they were clear enough to all.

'A favour, I beg you.'

Like everyone else, he riveted his eyes on her, and since he did not dismiss her plea she hurried on.

'It would give me right pleasure humbly to serve you. Only spare me, an' I'll be a hangman the like o' which was never yet seen in Roscommon. I'll prove it too, with these' — and her chained hands swung in an arc, like an invisible scythe cutting the legs of hope from beneath her companions in misery.

There were astounded looks for a moment, quickly turning to anger, then a growing chorus of growls, curses, snarls of outrage and hatred. But Betty's attention never wavered from the sheriff, and at length he smiled. Here, he realised, was a solution to his bother. Let her do as she proposed and this day's awkwardness would be ideally disposed of. Later, she herself could as conveniently be removed, if somewhat more privately.

He nodded, amused at his own subtlety, and beckoned to the turnkey, who immediately sprang to free her from her

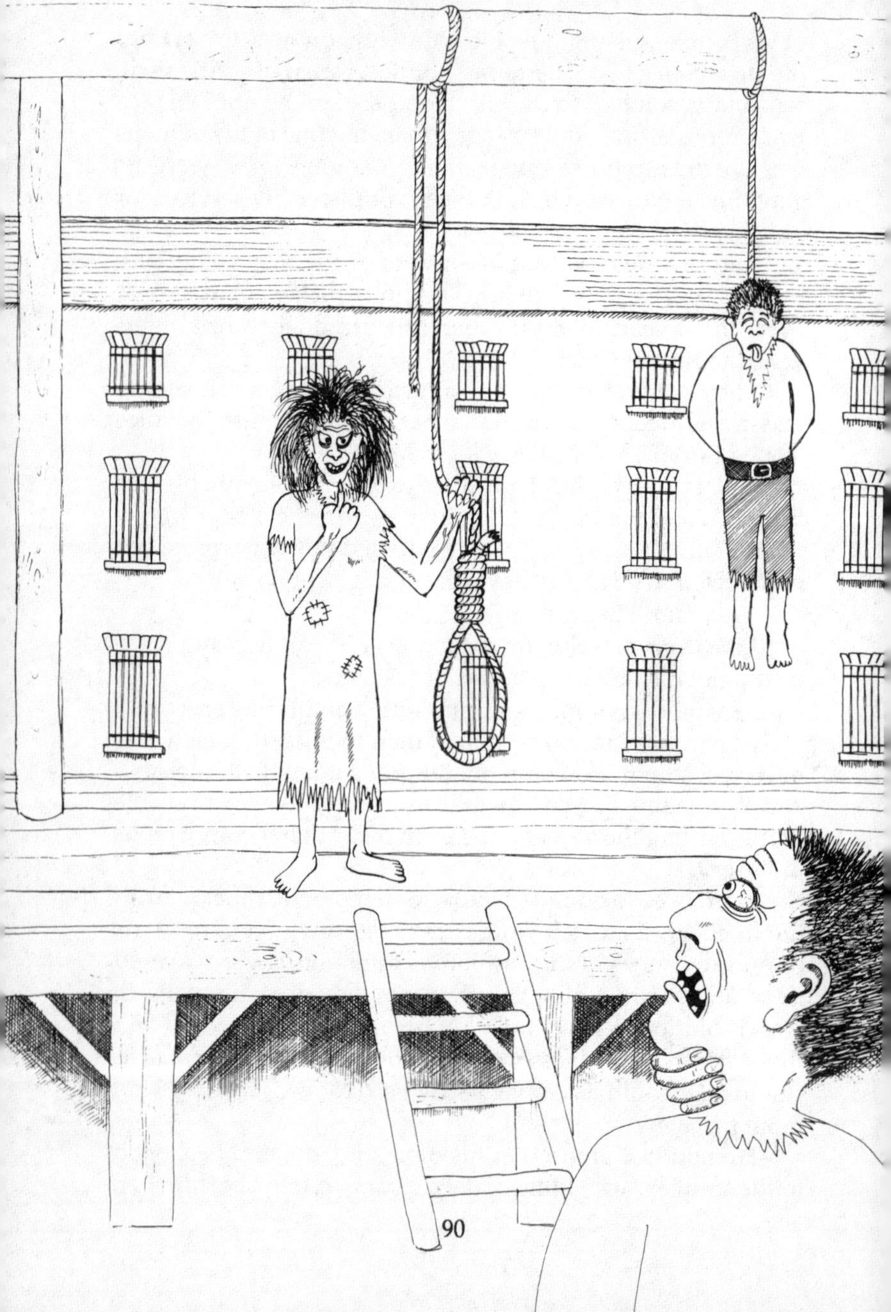

shackles. Grimly she fell out of that fatal line. Rubbing her wrists, she walked stolidly to the gallows, ascended the five rude steps that separated life from eternity. Without direction from the squeamish sheriff she grasped the nearest rope, adjusted it as if every refinement of that horrid trade were known to her. The crowd gaped, a single mouth now, as she beckoned the first of her erstwhile companions to her with a deadly earnest smile that chilled those who were close enough to observe it. Cringing, bug-eyed, he was man-handled up the steps, and as quickly despatched, Betty making up in enthusiasm for what she lacked in skill.

Even the sheriff felt a tightening in his stomach as he watched, fascinated, the dying kicks of the victim — as though he had never witnessed the like before.

A second, a third body was swivelling obscenely in public view before the true horror of it began to register with the onlookers. But by then it was too late. The soldiers had had time to prepare themselves and they stood to arms now, enjoying this entertainment where, for once, someone else was doing the killing. Some had even begun to bet on the toll Betty might exact, and no Irish rabble was going to be allowed hinder a fair bet! But Betty was conscious of nothing but the face of her son, his eyes glazing, the terrible bag of gold. All else was shadows, a flickering of strangely-dancing wraiths that noised and gestured but signified nothing.

So she worked relentlessly on, and when the final twitch of life had left the last poor stretched body, she looked out over the now-hushed throng, made the same gesture as once before, a slow scything sweep with her forefinger, from left to right and back again. Then she jabbed it to her own neck, drew it savagely across in a movement that no one could misunderstand: 'You too if ....'

She was escorted then, back to the jail. But the sheriff would not meet her, let alone speak to her. No one, in fact, congratulated her, even thanked her, for the service she had performed. But Betty had long since ceased to believe in niceties such as gratitude. What she hoped for, trusted in, was their need.

In that she was wise. A short time afterwards, news came that the hangman's illness was something more than a turn of conscience; in fact the poor man was dead. A replacement had to be found, and quickly, for already Roscommon jail had begun to fill again. But who? Who only she that had proved herself so adroit already! With a minimum of ceremony the unholy bargain was struck: on their side, a half-yearly salary and a guarantee of secure lodgings in the jail, as well as ongoing employment; on hers a vow to ask no questions, merely to execute the sentence of the courts. One precaution the authorities did take: Betty's sentence was not quashed, only suspended *sine die*. By this they thought to ensure her loyalty. Had they had the wit they might have seen that no such sanction was necessary, for she seemed at last to have found her true vocation.

She set to work with a relentless efficiency and quickly proved a resourceful, even an innovative functionary. No longer free to move safely about the town, even had she wanted to, she spent her days pacing the dank corridors of her new quarters, the straight grey walls simplifying wonderfully her view of life and lives, the dim light in each barred window a reminder of the one vision that she would never shake off: the light fading in his blue eyes. With a resignation removed only a hairs-breadth from hysteria she steeled herself, forced her thoughts into the narrowness of efficiency: if she must endlessly relive her deed, let it be done to some purpose. Better to act decisively in the hope that at least some waking hours might not be wasted.

It was she who first pointed out to the governor of the jail how dangerous it was to hold executions outside the walls in the market-place, putting the lives of his men needlessly at risk. He listened, though he was ill-disposed to accept any advice a woman might offer. Yet, it had often enough caused him nights of wakefulness, the official place of execution. But he had never summoned up enough wit to confront the problem. It was the knowledge of this that caused him to listen now.

"Twould be very aisy to rig up a handy little gallows here inside, your honour, if only you'd give the word to a couple o' masons. An' 'twould spare us all a lot o' bother.'

Masons? Carpenters he might have understood, but masons! The woman was obviously crazed.

Her shrewd eyes read his thoughts in his face. Her fingers shot upward, pointed to a rusted iron beam protruding from the wall thirty feet up.

'There, sir! Think, if a man was set to walk from there, would not the people have their lesson preached as well as from without the walls. An' no danger.'

He could not gainsay her words, though it would mean some alterations to the face of the building. But 'masons', she had said. He looked at her, sharply. She was smiling. And to his credit he had the wit to understand that here was one who knew her business more surely, perhaps, than he knew his. He turned away, not wishing more contact, maybe fearing it.

'See to that,' he flicked, glancing up as he strode off.

Betty did see to it, the breaking out of a doorway, the installing of a hinged horizontal floorspace on which the victim might stand a final brief time, the renewing of the beam overhead. No better foreman ever directed workmen than she and the task was completed well in time for the assizes' ritual clearing of the jail.

Betty excelled herself on the day, delighting in her speedy new arrangements, anxious to display them to best advantage. And with each neck that cracked as the bolt beneath the timberwork was whipped back, a snarl of anger and frustration went up from the spectators, who could clearly see the proceedings but could now not even aspire to intervene. Word somehow got out that these new arrangements were Betty's doing, but the public at large was in no way impressed by her ingenuity. And even though a steady trickle of strangers — even English visitors — began to appear in the town, looking to be shown the extraordinary new apparatus of dispatch, they were greeted with less than customary Irish civility. The townspeople shrank from such publicity; even those who might have profited from the curious travellers dared not seem too enthusiastic.

Betty, with every assize that passed, burned her presence deeper and deeper into the consciousness of the town. She became a bugbear, a serious rival to the *púca* as a terroriser of children at bedtime, a close relation of the banshee herself. And all the time she was there among them, though secretly, practically unseen. The stories multiplied, fuelled by personal 'authentic' accounts from those whose tenancy in the jail had been less than fatal. They had seen her apartment, they said, a spacious suite, equipped with every device of torture invented by the sinful mind of man. Some swore she drank poitín from the skull of one of her victims, others that she had taken to decorating the walls with a grisly tally of the likenesses of those she executed. None of the accounts was much diminished in the retelling. Yet, though all of them differed, the faith of sensible men, those who might have been prepared to allow her the benefit of any doubt, was prostrated by each passing assize, and the gusto which she displayed for her task of termination.

Never was this more obvious than in the troubled days of the Whiteboy agitation, for not alone was she called on to break the neck of rebellion; she was also given a new responsibility: that of banishing rebellious tendencies from those the law judged to be guilty, but not capitally so. Her weapons were the lash and cat, though once she had mastered the niceties of these she began to experiment, to inquire into what other methods there might be of removing skin from backs and buttocks in whatever quantities required. Hazel did well, she found, briar not as well as its appearance would suggest; but most reliable of all was the common sally rod so beloved of basket-makers. A judiciously-chosen specimen in sensitive hands might outlast two hundred skins and still retain its sting.

From this time, a change became noticeable in Betty.

From one who estimated her worth by how many she could separate from their lives in the shortest possible time, she came to savour the delicate degrees of pain that flogging might be made to yield. It is doubtful whether her victims shared in much of the pleasure! To the terror and humiliation of these poor wretches was now added the burden of Betty's growing and obsessive perfectionism. To be found guilty in Roscommon shortly became synonymous with either speedy dispatch or lingering half-death. Little wonder that Whiteboyism and other symptoms of agrarian discontent soon withered and died within her jurisdiction. Nor did they revive even in the Year of Liberty, 1798. Betty's thoroughness saw to that. So confident of her deterrent powers had the authorities become that even during this time of mortal danger her request that she be half-retired was granted. Her name and reputation inspired more fear now than her hand, and well her masters knew it.

The new century dawned, darkness or light depending on the class and creed of the beholder. Great, though insidious, changes were in the offing, but in Roscommon so unruffled was the public mind by either crime or politics that even sheep-stealing, traditionally of epidemic proportions in the region, had become the rage of conversation by virtue of its very absence. Mutton, it seems, had lost its appeal in face of Betty's skinning-techniques.

By now, the rate of executions in the county had dropped so alarmingly as to become the subject of suspicious enquiries from the servants of the crown in Dublin Castle. Most assuredly, reasoned those cynical functionaries, the homicidal Irish peasant could not have changed. Therefore, either a large and as yet incomprehensible conspiracy was afoot, or the sheriff was grossly neglecting his duty. He was summoned to account for his presumed misdeeds, but he took the precaution of having Betty accompany him. She, he felt, would be his trump card. She was that, indeed, and much more, for those dried-up, legalistic men demanded proof of her miraculous skills. There was no lack of subjects on which to prove her effectiveness, and their hearts began to beat faster, blood almost flowed in their veins again as they beheld the thoroughness of her preparations for both hanging and flaying. With growing admiration they watched as she effortlessly went about her business, then saw it through to the last twitch, the last drop of blood.

One hardened old martinet was heard to mutter as she bowed herself out, 'By Gad, the Admiralty might do worse than employ such a one' — for the mutinies at Spithead and the Nore of five years before were still seething in the minds of those with much to lose by the rising-up of trampled working-men.

After such a display, the rest of the inquiry was a mere formality. They returned to Roscommon in triumph, the sheriff with a written commendation in his pocket. Betty had even greater cause to rejoice: her death-sentence of all those years before had at last been lifted, put aside by special intervention of the Lord Lieutenant himself in recognition of her preservation of the public safety in Roscommon during dangerous times. Now she could retire in peace. And so she did, though the fact was not advertised.

She died peacefully in 1807, tending her little garden within the jail precincts, and was buried secretly and by night on the sheriff's express orders. No marker was permitted on her last resting-place. Any such might have undone all the work of her diligent hands over the years, perhaps have unleashed an avalanche of crime and mayhem. It was better for all that she should be supposed still alive and threatening. Thus, even from her grave she kept the peace, haunted the minds of young and old alike for almost a generation more. Not until well into the 1820s did crime raise a timid head again in Roscommon, and even today, when normality in that regard has been fully restored, mention of her name can still bring a lull to conversation, a nervous shifting of eyes towards dark corners.

In her native Kerry fate has been more – or less? – kind; her name, her very existence, has been long ago forgotten.

4

Spioraid na mBearnan

In the bad times, long before the Great Famine spread silence over the countryside of west Limerick, there lived in the parish of Templeglantine a family named Shaughnessy at a place called Barna. Here it is that the heights of Kerry gather themselves to look down on the plain about New-castlewest, and so suddenly does the road rise that travellers to the Kingdom of Kerry always regarded it as a test of their strength or the strength of their horses. So hard and steep was the climb that Barna became the chief obstacle on all that lonely highway, a place to be regarded with foreboding. But there was another reason, too, why those who passed here should cast their eyes nervously about as they struggled uphill, especially as evening shadows crept across the little fields. For this was the haunt of Moll Shaughnessy, 'the Spirit of Barna', a ferocious creature who exacted a bloody toll from all who passed by during the hours of night.

How she came to this horrible state is yet in the memories of old people of that place, a story to give pause even to the motorised traveller of today. For who knows, glancing in your rear-view mirror as you slow to pass the gaunt pillars of the old railway-bridge, who is to say you may not notice a pair of eyes other than your own staring back at you? Hold the wheel steady at that moment, for if once you stop or lose control you are at her mercy. And you will by no means be the first to have felt those icy fingers sinking slowly, irresist-ibly into your neck ... blotting out the moonlight and all other light ... forever.

As to the Shaughnessy family, however, they were miserably poor. Like most others of the Irish in that place they scratched out a living from a small rushy farm, and to help pay the rent on the gale-days Patrick Shaughnessy

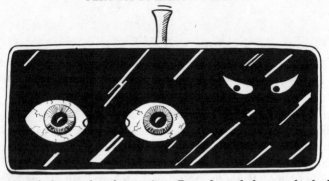

practised the trade of weaving. But, though he worked all the hours of daylight that God sent, there never seemed to be enough food on the table for his growing young family, and more than once he had had to grovel before the landlord's agent, beg for more time to scrape the rent money together. There was no help for it. Such was the nature of things in the Ireland of those days.

To make all worse, Patrick Shaughnessy's family consisted of four daughters, a sore worry for the poor man, because where would he get dowries for them, so that they might marry? Ireland was no kind place at that time for penniless girls. Money in the fist was better thought of than love in the heart, and many a young life was thwarted to serve the ancient needs of gold.

The second daughter, Mary, was a handsome girl and, from her youngest days, independent of mind. Headstrong, the older women of the place called her, and warned her more than once that she would never get a man unless she changed her way of looking at the world. And always she would reply, quietly, as if measuring something in her own mind, 'Get a man! Yes, indeed.'

Time passed, and as Mary grew into womanhood she began to notice that her father was no longer the strong man she had known. Ceaseless work had worn him so that he seemed to be shrinking, fading away. Now, as he came home in the evenings, bending under the weight of rushes he had cut along the hillside, he seemed almost a dwarf, like one of the Good People — though she would never have dared to say so aloud. But it was obvious to her that if she were to get a man, as the older women said, she would have to do so herself. Her father would never have five sovereigns to rub together, let alone the fifty it would take to hook any half-reasonable husband.

She began to look about her. And in no long time she fixed her bright eyes on a young man of many acres. If the same young man had a humped back and sight in only one eye, what of it? She noticed none of it. Love is blind, after all. Yet, she saw clearly enough the extent of his fields, how solid was his house, and the delightful fact that he had no old father and mother to burden him. And so she knew happiness of a sort. Her parents were content too, for though he might not look everything a son-in-law should, Mary's future seemed secure — and many such match had been known to turn out happily in the past, with God's help and a little understanding.

A weight seemed to have been lifted from the mind of Patrick Shaughnessy. He was even seen to smile on occasion now, and appeared less hopeless than for many a day. He, as much as Mary, was looking forward to the wedding as a way out of the poverty that had always been with them.

A date was set, arrangements were made with the priest, and all was put in order for a memorable celebration. Everything was done that should be done and all seemed set for a satisfactory ending. Sometimes, however, plans go astray. They did so now, for on the morning of the wedding, Mary, for no known reason, changed her mind. She would *not* go to the church, she said, even though the bridegroom was there already, prepared and waiting.

Her mother spoke reasonably to her, remembering her own nerves on a similar day twenty-eight years before.

'But, Mary, *a chroí*, isn't it a bit late to be talking this way now? You had right to tell us before this. Sure, you can't leave the poor man standing like a fool there at the altar.'

'I *can*, and I will!'

The poor mother could do nothing to change Mary's mind, so she went to Patrick, who was conferring with the priest, to report how matters stood. At first he did not believe her.

'No time for joking, woman. Come on! His reverence here is waiting.'

'There'll be no come on,' she said. 'Mary has her mind changed. She won't marry him.'

Now that he saw there was no joke, he was not pleased. With clenched fists and jaw set dangerously he called Mary to him.

'What's this I hear? What oul' nonsense is in your head this morning that you won't marry him?'

The priest stood by nodding gravely. It was obvious where his sympathies lay.

'I could never be happy with a man like that, father. There's no ...'

'Happy? Who said anything about being happy?' He was genuinely shocked at her innocence. ''Tis to get married you're going, girl. You can be happy after if you like, but you're going to the church now!'

'I'm not! I won't do it!'

He was mortified. His own daughter to talk like this, in front of the priest, too. 'You will!' he spat. 'Or else you'll walk the roads from this day out, you brazen hussy. Oh, what kind of a daughter did you rear at all, woman?'

If the poor mother had any opinions on that matter, she kept them to herself, because the priest was again nodding, disapproving. He spoke now, solemn, sensible talk.

'Mary! Mary! Think again. Remember your poor father and mother and all they have done for you. If you refuse now, think of the scandal. It could break their hearts.'

''Tis me that'll break *her* back if she doesn't walk out that door this minute an' walk on to that fine man that's waiting for her. Glad she should be to get the like of him. Go on! An' smile!'

She had little choice. With parents and priest against her,

she was forced to marry the man she had so rashly chosen. And certainly they looked an ill-matched pair as they received the priest's blessing. But at least they had the good wishes of most of the neighbours, if that counted for anything. It was a subdued wedding-feast that followed the ceremony, and an even more sombre homecoming. Mary was not in a mood for talk.

Who should wonder at it if that marriage failed to prosper? Things most oft bad begun most oft get worse, as a wise man once said. And so it was. The husband, in a short time, when he could get no response from Mary, began to measure his own disability against her beauty. What he saw made him angry, then bitter. She, for her part, lost all patience with his constant carping, and soon there was more silence than talk in that handsome house. He began to take to other company for consolation, then to drink in order to dull his sorrows. And there was no shortage of drinking companions to advise him what to do about his unreasonable wife. Under these influences, his behaviour became violent, his moods unpredictable, and all the while his resentment against Mary grew stronger.

Then fate took one of its unpredictable twists. One Saturday evening he came home raving drunk as she was busy about the pots and pans at the fire. Even before she saw him, she heard his shouts of abuse from the yard. Anger and fear flared up in her and when, moments later, he drove in the door, cursing and threatening to kill her, a violent spasm gripped her. Without so much as a thought, she swung around, struck him straight between the eyes with the tongs and stretched him senseless and bleeding on the kitchen flagstones.

Horrified, she realised what she had done. The tongs clattered to the ground from her numbed fingers. She sank to her knees, felt his pulse. Nothing! Overcome with shock she fainted. If anyone had entered the kitchen at that moment it might have appeared to him the scene of some horrible slaughter. In fact it was exactly that, though all unintended.

Presently Mary was faced with the likely consequences of her act. As soon as she recovered her wits she saw that the body must be got rid of. And an answer soon presented itself to her, competent woman that she was. She decided to cut him into pieces and to bury him bit by bit here and there about the farm. Luckily for her, she had had previous experience at this kind of operation, for on many occasions pigs had been killed at home, cut up and barrelled in salt. Barrel and salt she dispensed with on this occasion. She was glad enough to dispose of the limbs wherever was convenient so long as they were out of the house. She wanted nothing more to do with her husband or any part of him. That night she went stealthily about her gruesome business, and by dawn all was hidden except for the head, with its twisted face still wrenched in the shocked position of its moment of death. This deserved special treatment, and Mary Shaughnessy saw to it that it was scanted no honour — she buried it in the dung-heap in the yard: 'You had ever a dirty mouth, husband, and now you have something to fill it with,' said she.

But, of course the man was missed, especially by his drinking companions. They came to the house, enquiring for him, but little courtesy did Mary extend to them: 'Ye have the cheek to come to me! Ye're the ones he carouses with, ye idle wasters. If I had my way 'tis transportation ye'd get. An' too good for the likes of ye it'd be!' And she slammed the door in their faces.

Her parents were not so easily put off, but them too she answered coldly: 'How should I know where he is? If he chooses to spend day and night from home, how can I help it?'

Days passed into weeks and inevitably the law was called on — but not by Mary — to lend its heavy hand to the search for the missing man. One morning a group of soldiers appeared in Mary's yard, their red coats brilliant in the early sunlight, bloodhounds straining on leashes before them.

The officer, a handsome lieutenant, stepped smartly into the kitchen, took in the surroundings at a glance. Fine place, he thought. Comfortable. Fine woman, too.

'We have reason to believe, madam,' he said, 'that your husband may have met with foul play. We have been sent to conduct a search.'

A thrill of horror struck Mary dumb for an instant. Had they found out? But though she was unable to rise, she somehow held her composure, even managed to speak steadily: 'Do you think, sir, that *I* have not searched? But I wish you success.'

She could trust herself to say no more, so closely was the officer eyeing her. But it was admiration, not accusation, that was in his gaze. Here, if ever, was a time and place for a cursory search. And who could tell, maybe a private visit at another time might be appreciated! He smiled, tipped his hat and bowed himself out.

'Pardon our intrusion, madam. We shall be gone in minutes.'

But now fate took another, and fatal, twist, for just as the lieutenant called his men to leave, there was a burst of yelping from near the dungheap. The handler of one of the hounds was struggling to drag his charge away from that reeking mass, but the dog would have none of it.

'What ails the cur?' shouted the lieutenant, angry to be jolted out of his pleasant daydream.

'Something here, sir, whatever it be.'

'Aye, dung. Any fool may see that. The brute's senses are astray. Drag him off, man. And let us be away.'

The hound was burrowing now, however, sending spatters flying out behind her, baying furiously all the while. The handler aimed a kick at her, but the blow never fell for the dog was tugging at something that looked horribly like hair. The soldier stooped, looked closer and recoiled, holding his nose and mouth.

'Pahh! Sir! Sir! Look here.'

The excitement in his voice drew the others in a rush,

and there, staring from the dung, they saw the sightless eye-sockets of Mary Shaughnessy's husband. The lieutenant turned aside from the babble of his men. All at once, at the whim of a dog's nose, his pleasurable fantasy had been shattered. He glanced towards the door of the house, regret fading to resignation; then, collecting himself, he issued a string of abrupt orders: 'Dig out that vile mess! Search those barns! And two of you, come with me.'

All that was done, much to the disgust of the soldiers, so proud of their spotless uniforms. And, meanwhile, the lieutenant, having stationed the two guards at the door, entered the kitchen once more. Mary still sat, motionless, in the same chair. Well she knew what the dog's howlings signified.

The lieutenant looked her over, slowly. 'So, lady, it seems that you are other than you appear. A pity,' he added. 'For now you must accompany us, and I fear it will go heavy with you.'

She was escorted to Limerick, brought before a magistrate and accused of her husband's murder. Freely did she admit that she had caused his death, but she denied fiercely that it was murder. At the trial she held to this, said that she had been provoked. Yet, though the man on the bench was no Judge Jeffreys, he had little scope for mercy, so rigid was the law.

'Even though others are as much at fault in this as you are, still must I pass the heaviest sentence of the law. A poor example it would be to other wives to let you loose. Have you a last and reasonable request?'

Her only wish, she said, was to see her home in Barna one last time. She would be happy to quit life there, if that might be.

It pleased his Lordship to grant her as much, and so she was brought back and hanged in her own yard. It was such humane touches that kept English law so fondly-regarded among the common people of Ireland at that time!

With the snapping of her neck, Mary lost all interest in the doings of this world, temporarily, at least. In an eye-

blink she was at the doors of heaven, or some doors suspiciously like them. But the doors were locked, and all was in silence. Collecting her courage, she knocked, and knocked again. No response. She hammered louder. Still no reply. She began to shout, ever more urgently, and when she had given up and was on the point of turning away, a little window to one side squealed open. An old man poked out his head, eyed her blearily.

'Who are you, an' what d'you want?'

'I want to go in. That's all,' she cried.

'Wait!' he croaked, and slammed the window to. Trembling, she waited. After what seemed eternity the right-hand of the huge pair of doors moved a fraction, and the grey head appeared again.

'What d'you want?'it asked.

'I told you, I want to go in.'

'Where're you from?'

'West Limerick.'

'Hurghhh!' It sounded like a strangled laugh. 'We have no one from that place here. What name are you?'

'Shaughnessy, but I was married to ...'

'I know all about that,' he mumbled sourly. 'You didn't make much of a hand of it, did you?'

That stung her. 'You needn't blame me. It wasn't all my fault!'

He said no more, only reached into a little alcove and tugged out a heavy tattered ledger. He flicked through its well-thumbed pages, searched at a particular place, then thumped it shut.

'No one of that name on our books. Sorry, but best to be going.'

'Going? Where can I go?'

'Back to Barna, where you came from! That's where. You are condemned,' said he, 'by the blood you shed,' and then, as if anticipating her reply, 'but, as you say, you are not wholly to blame. The greater guilt for your husband's death lies with your father and the priest. And they will suffer for it, never fear.'

And so they did. Patrick Shaughnessy died roaring a few weeks after his daughter's hanging, and the priest, on his way to a funeral that autumn, was thrown from his horse and broke his neck. Little did he realise that morning that it was his own funeral he was setting out for!

Nevertheless, that was little consolation to poor Mary, trapped as she was so near to, yet so far from, heaven. She begged again to be let in, but though she knelt and wrung her hands, she found, oddly, that she could not weep.

'Silence!' snapped the impatient old voice of the grey-beard. 'Hold your whist, and listen. Punished you must be, and near to where the deed was done, a daily reminder to you of the blood you spilt. Begone to Barna, and remain there till some brave or foolish mortal does battle with you fearlessly and lives to tell the tale.'

The door snapped shut and Mary found herself falling, falling ....

And so at last she came home, and went to work immediately, to terrify each and every passer by that place. Thoroughly she did her job, too, for a century and more. And in all that time no one spoke to her a solitary word. They were, one and all, too busy trying to escape her clutching fingers or flashing white fangs — for as well as appearing in her own shape she was sometimes seen as a hound, snow-white except for a black tip at the end of her tail. *Spioraid na mBearnan* they called her, a name that travelled the length and breadth of Munster, carrying fear and dread with it. So evil a reputation did Barna acquire that no one familiar with her doings would ever dare to venture that way after dark. Seven, eight miles out of their way they would walk, even in the worst of winter weather, rather than face the certainty of her deathly-cold fingers on their windpipes. But still the victims came, for not all strangers had heard of her.

Yet, in all her long reign of horror, only once did she

meet an opponent who was even half worthy of her. That was during the building of the railway in the 1850s. In those hungry years labouring men came from far and near, glad of the employment that the works provided. Among their number was a man from Mountcollins. A giant even among his burly fellow-workers, he could lift a rail in either hand and lay them two by two on the waiting sleepers, almost a one-man crane. Steadily the works crept upward from the valley; day after day they drew nearer to the lair of Spioraid na mBearnan. Perhaps she was alarmed at the encroachment of the steam age; or maybe she welcomed the prospect of new victims. Whatever the case, a clash was bound to come, and it did. The giant from Mountcollins, rather than walk the twelve miles to and from the works each day, had built himself a little hut of boards, roughly thatched with rushes, at Gortnagloss, and there he lived the six working days from Monday to Saturday, returning home only on Sunday for Mass and to see his parents. His friends chaffed him, of course:

'Where are you burying the gold, Liam? Are you saving up the fare for America, or what?' But they knew better than to rouse his anger, and so the joking remained a friendly affair, the kind of banter to liven a lunchtime break.

Then, on a day when the embankment for the first and lower of the Barna bridges was being topped off, a workman from the town of Newcastlewest, one who had a low regard for 'country goms', piped up, 'Wisha, Liam, isn't it a wonder you aren't afraid to stay in that oul' *bothán* of a hut by night? You'd want to mind yourself, or Spioraid na mBearnan'll get you. I'm thinking even yourself'd hardly be able for her.'

He laughed, in a way that everyone might hear, and then returned to his picking.

For a moment there was silence, then a rumble of a reply: 'I have five sovereigns here to say I'll take her on wherever she chooses.'

An even longer silence greeted this piece of news. Faces, startled at first, then breaking into grins, turned towards the townsman, a taunt in each and every one. His joke had been turned, his bluff called. Though every man of them knew that he could not possibly afford such a huge bet, they also knew he could not now back out.

'All right!' said he, trying to put a confident front on necessity. 'All right. If you'll walk up and down this hill every night next week, an' if you meet her an' take her on, I'll pay you the five pounds.' But then he laughed slyly. 'I shouldn't make a bargain like this, though, 'cos I'll never collect, even if I win.'

'How so?' they asked. 'Are you making a liar out o' Liam?'

'Indeed I'm not. But, sure, even if he fights her itself, he won't live to tell the story.'

No more was said. The following Monday the bets were collected and held by the foreman, and that evening, when work was done, Liam began his solitary vigil, refusing all offers of company from his friends. It was his fight, he said, no one else's. They knew better than to argue.

Monday night passed uneventful, as did the dark hours of Tuesday and Wednesday. Relief began to spread through the work-site. Some were even heard to mock the very notion of Spioraid na mBearnan's existence: 'Begod, if she was in it, she'd be seen by now.'

Liam, if he noticed this change, gave no sign. He was like a man engaged in a holy duty, impervious. At knocking-off time on the Thursday he returned to his hut while the others scattered, each to his own destination. A witness was later to swear that he saw Liam emerge from the little shack at about seven o'clock, but what happened after that is anyone's guess.

When the men came to work on Friday morning a scene of destruction greeted them: furze bushes and young trees uprooted and scattered over the hillsides of Gortnagloss, large chunks of earth torn out of the sides of the embankment, metal rails bent and buckled in impossible shapes for three hundred yards down the hill. But of Liam there was no trace. Men formed into search-parties and hastened in all directions, but they had not far to seek. They found him in his little hut, moaning feebly, a few tattered pieces of cloth clinging to him. But what gave them pause was the pattern of ugly weals and welts that criss-crossed his body from head to foot. Medical aid was rushed to him, but though he was transferred at once to Newcastle workhouse he survived only two days. His death, according to the inquest verdict, had been caused by some kind of whip, but any more than that they could not say for sure.

The old people of Barna, had anyone asked their opinion, would have quickly solved the mystery. Well they knew that Spioraid na mBearnan had whipped Liam to death with her tail — the tail with the deadly black tip. Had she not been for generations, in her playful moments, levelling their hay and potatoes by the self-same method?

The ten sovereigns were sent to Liam's parents in Mountcollins, a poor enough payment for his death, and a collection among his fellow-workers on the railway amounted to four pounds more, which was spent on Masses for his eternal rest.

The remainder of the railway along Barna hill and on to Templeglantine was completed in record time, the workers being most anxious to see the last of that bleak place. And, with the fading of the clatter and chime of their picks and hammers, Barna returned to its brooding air of silence and menace, and the highway was left to the cruel keeping of Mary Shaughnessy, as before.

However, all things have an end at last. One stormy November night, a generation later, a poor shoemaker called John Ahearne, from Inchebawn, was hurrying that way. His wife had been dangerously sick all that day and, coming on darkness, John's neighbours begged him to go to Newcastlewest for Dr Moynihan. Otherwise she would be dead before morning. Truly, he was in no condition to ride, so confused and excited was he, but they got him a loan of a saddle-horse and told him to waste no time. Then, just as he was on the point of launching forth from the yard, an old man snatched the reins.

'Are you not forgetting something, John?'

Poor John could hardly reply, so distracted was he. 'Lord God,' he said, 'I hardly know what I'm doing this night. What is it, at all?'

'This!' cried the old one, handing up one of John's sharp leather-knives. 'You might want it when you're passing Barna. *Herself* could be there to block you!'

John looked stupidly for a few seconds at the weapon, then tucked it into a pouch by the saddle and galloped off without another word.

In the frenzy of half-thoughts that surged through his mind as he pounded over the dark countryside, Mary Shaughnessy was soon forgotten. Only as he crossed the heights of Barna and began the steep descent towards the town did the old man's warning grasp at him again, and that most violently. At one moment he was urging his horse on, begging the animal to go faster; the next, his voice was abruptly choked off by a collar of icy fingers. Recognition came to him instantly — Spioraid na mBearnan! Struggling to keep his balance and his senses, he groped for the knife in the saddle-pouch. But, to his consternation, it was gone. Had she somehow sensed the danger to herself and removed it, or had he lost it in his mad dash along the narrow roads? It hardly mattered now. All that concerned him was staying alive. Terror lent him strength, but the same terror caused the horse to rear, mouth foaming, hooves flailing. John was flung awkwardly into the drain by the roadside, but injured or not, he scrambled up and tried to run for it. It was a forlorn effort. She was on him again almost at once, nails tearing, grim mouth smiling a terrible smile.

It was an unequal battle from the beginning and, in no

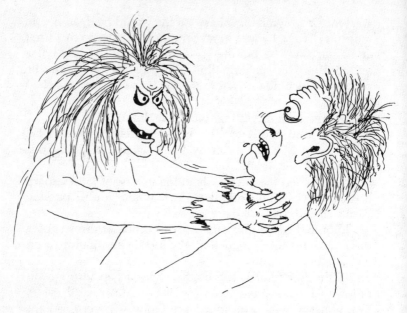

more than a few minutes, John was at her mercy, sunk back in the drain again, her iron hands squeezing his life away. He was convinced his last moments had come. But then, remembering his sick wife at home, he made a last attempt to loosen her grip enough to croak out a few words. That he succeeded was due, perhaps, to the prayers of some unknown benefactor; but succeed he did. He spoke her name: 'Please! Please, Mary Shaughnessy, for the honour of God, leave me my life, on this night above all nights.' He thought he detected a flicker in those baneful eyes, a tiny slackening of her grip. 'My wife is sick, maybe dying at this very minute. I'm going for the doctor. Only let me do that an' I'll come back ... I'll do whatever you tell me to. I won't fail you, whatever else.'

Somewhere in that cold heart a spark of humanity obviously remained alight, a flicker of sympathy for a suffering fellow-woman. She relaxed her hold on his neck and, for the first time in mortal memory, she spoke. Cracked and gravelly her words sounded to his shivering senses, but her message was crystal clear: 'For now, go! But be back in this place at this time a week from tonight.'

He thanked her again and again, bowed himself out of her presence — still fearful to turn his back! — and rushed helter-skelter down the hill. He found his horse grazing a mile away, clawed himself into the saddle and never slackened his pace until he arrived in Doctor Moynihan's yard, almost in as much need of that gentleman's help as was his wife. The good doctor was none too pleased to be disturbed at that late hour, and even less so at the prospect of facing Barna. But John somehow assured him that they would not be harmed, and finally he reluctantly agreed to go.

They travelled silently and fast, arrived safely and in time to save the sick woman, but the doctor, rather than face Barna alone, stayed until daylight, claiming, of course, that the patient was still too unwell to be left to unskilled hands. No one in that relieved company begrudged him his opinion.

However, now that the immediate danger had been dealt with, John Ahearne's promise began to loom larger and more frightening with every hour that passed. What was he to do? To break his word, to run, to hide — all these occurred to him and were dismissed. She would find him, no matter where he hid.

It began to keep him from his sleep. But no matter how he paced, no matter what twists and turns his mind attempted, like a hare seeking escape from greyhounds, he could see no solution. At last, in desperation, two days before the pernicious date, he went to the parish priest and told all.

'Oh, poor man,' replied the reverend, 'that was a hard promise to have to make.'

'But, Father, what could I do! It was either that or my wife's life.'

'I know that. I know that, John,' and he pondered for a while in silence. Hope had begun to sink a little in John's mind when the older man spoke again.

'You have to keep your promise. That much is clear. But if you go back there alone ....'

'I know well what's going to happen, Father. I looked into her eyes once already an' I know what's there. But now, if someone like yourself was with me ...'

The priest chuckled, a humourless little snuffle. 'Do you think, John, that if I could be of any help to you I wouldn't have offered to go without being asked? But it wouldn't serve. The only chance you have against Moll Shaughnessy is to get a newly-ordained priest, one who hasn't a Mass said in public yet. He's your only hope.'

To John it sounded like a death-sentence. 'Where am I going to find a person like that in the two days I have left?' he almost wailed.

'I might be able to help you, John. Leave it with me an' I'll see what I can do.'

A day and a half passed without word or sign, a time of torture for John. Then, late on the fateful evening, by which time he had long resigned himself to facing Barna alone, a fast horse-trap pulled up before the parochial house and a young man, dressed in black, dismounted and entered, carrying a small case. Within the hour, John was summoned and introduced to the stranger. There was little to be said, for the parish priest had already done the necessary explaining, and after a few final instructions he sent them on their way with a blessing. Few words were spoken on that moonlit journey. It was not a time for talk, even of a casual kind.

Near the hill at last, they tethered the horse in a disused quarry close by the railway bridge and made their way cautiously forward. The young priest fumbled in his fob, snapped open his pocket-watch.

'Ten minutes to twelve,' he announced tersely, not quite able to conceal the apprehensiveness in his voice. 'Point out the place.'

John did so, fascinated by the uncontrollable shake in his finger.

At once, the young man went to work. In the steely half-light he took from his coat pockets a large leather-bound prayer book and a bottle. A third, bulky object he kept hidden. John could dimly trace its outline, but he asked no questions, only glanced around nervously, willing his companion to hurry with whatever it was he was doing. The priest uncorked the bottle.

'You know what this is?' he whispered. 'Holy water. Our protection against all evil. Stand still now, like a good man.' And he made three concentric circles with the water on the roadway, with John standing in the innermost.

'Whatever else you do now, don't stir from there. If you do, I can't help you.' He moved a few yards to one side then, made a single circle round himself, and began silently to arrange his bookmarkers at the selected prayers.

Presently they heard a sound high in the glen overhead, a trampling noise, as of a heavy animal moving through undergrowth. Tingling in every nerve they strained to see. And then, it burst from the height above them, a huge hound, blue-white in the moonlight. Agile as a cat, it pounced, landed in the roadway between them, and with a menacing glare at the priest, pawed its way soundlessly towards John Ahearne. He shook in every limb, might have collapsed in sheer terror, had not the priest begun at that moment to read from his book. As if stung, the spectre bounded towards her victim, teeth showing through ugly wrinkled lips. But though she got her nose past the outer circle of holy water, she could go no further. Snarling, she leaped back, then flung herself again towards John. He cringed, but the priest read on. A second time she almost reached her quarry, but this time she failed to pass the middle circle. The priest neither slackened nor speeded the pace of his reading all the while, and the hound, with a shrill yelp of bafflement, sprang towards John a third time. Through both outer circles her leap carried her, but she was brought up sharp an inch from his throat, for the priest was behind, prayers finished, his foot stamped firmly on the black tip of her tail. Thwarted, tormented, she struggled to turn, but the priest's voice, confident now, rang out to the listening night:

'Spioraid na mBearnan, your day is done, and your power is at an end.'

Before their eyes she began to change, to take on the shape of a person, a woman — the very one, John knew, that had spared his life a week before. The eyes were the same, and he was afraid, maybe ashamed, to look into them now.

'Here!' cried the priest. 'Take this'— pulling from his pocket a cup, but no ordinary cup; the bottom had been cleanly knocked out — 'and go to Lough Gur. Empty that lake with this cup, and when you have that done, beat yourself black and blue with a one-ended stick as a penance for your sins. An' if you survive that, go an' wash your wounds in a river that flows uphill only. Never again show your face here in Barna until you complete these tasks!'

There was no escape for Spioraid na mBearnan. With a shriek she disappeared towards Lough Gur, a ball of fire in the night sky. And she must still be trying to empty that lake, because she was never seen in Barna from that day to this.

Effigy, said to be that of Spioraid na mBearnan (courtesy of M. O'Dwyer, Dromline).

5

ALICE KYTELER

In Ireland, unlike other countries, it has never been the custom to burn those suspected of witchcraft or wizardry. One of the very few such cases happened in Kilkenny some time before the Black Death — in the year 1324 to be precise.

At that time a woman named Alice Kyteler lived in the town, a notable woman, and of very respectable people, too. They were bankers and, from an early age, she showed herself so shrewd and quick-witted that her father took the unusual step of bringing her each day to his counting house to learn what she might, if she chose. There it was that she discovered the power and comfort money could bring, lessons that were to serve her for good — and evil. Something else she discovered too in her father's bank: that she was attractive to men. And as the years went by and her features shaped themselves into beauty of a threatening sort, the suitors gathered. At sixteen, her first husband was carefully chosen for her by her doting father. Ill-luck it was for her that her parent's judgment was not as clear as hers. The new bridegroom quickly showed himself to have more interest in Alice's fortune than in her person. Not that he ever got to spend too much of it. He lived only six months a married man, and scarcely in wedded bliss. The decline that claimed him at last was caused, some said, as much by lack of gold as by any physical ailment. But that was mere idle chatter, perhaps. The only certainty was that his married life was very brief and none too happy.

Three more husbands followed in quick succession, but only one child was born of all this frenzy of marrying, a son, William. To him Lady Alice became devoted, even to the neglect of her ageing parents, a circumstance noted well by the more prying among the citizens of the town. Rumours began to spread, that more than natural causes were to blame for the four untimely deaths. Rumours are ugly creatures at any time, since no one knows where they may begin or end, but when mention of witchcraft entwines itself with rumour, they unite to become dangerous and sinister.

It began to be whispered in the alleyways, on the street-corners of Kilkenny, that Dame Kyteler was dabbling in the deep waters of the Black Art. It was also said that at odd hours of day and night a tall dark man was seen visiting her house. Art Artisson they called him, and the more daring even hinted that young William might at length be found to be the son of no earthly father. Their thoughts were clear: it was none other than the Devil himself who had taken to visiting her.

For a woman of such wealth and standing, it was also thought odd that she employed only one servant, a woman, Petronilla of Meath by name. Why should this be, when ladies who were indeed only half-ladies were vying with each other to show off the numbers of their menials? Willy-nilly, poor Petronilla was drawn into the speculation surrounding her mistress, and though she did her best to lead a normal life, she could not but be aware of the dark mutterings and sidelong looks that greeted her every appearance in shop or market-place.

As of yet, however, there was no outcry or open confrontation. Lady Alice was a woman of many friends, some in high places too, and woe betide the speaker of scandal who could not support words of accusation with proofs. For the moment the neighbours' only recourse was to avoid both mistress and servant, or if they had to speak to either, to use as few words as possible. No one wanted to be smirched by the rumours, whatever might be the outcome of it all.

On May morning of the year 1324, one of these neighbours, a man living across from her house in Kieran Street, sat up in his bed with a start, just before dawn, and cocked his ears in the darkness.

'Very strange,' he muttered to himself, for he thought he had heard voices and some odd scraping noise. He listened, scratching himself and yawning. There it was again, the talking! He rose quickly and slipped from under the bedclothes.

'God knows,' he growled, 'how early some miscreants choose to hold their conversation beneath my window.'

He padded across the floor, opened the shutters a fraction and peeped through. And a strange sight he saw, for there, fully dressed in all her finery, was his neighbour, Dame Alice. But even more peculiar was her occupation, for she was performing a task that no lady would wish to be seen at: wielding a large kitchen broom and brushing the cobbles of the street. The man was too astonished even to speak. He continued there, staring at her, opening the shutters a little wider now, for she was moving off down the far side of the street, chanting something in a low voice. He almost laughed. Perhaps it was some penance laid on her by the good priests at St Canice's cathedral. He, like everyone else, had heard the rumours of witchcraft murmured against her.

Here she came, along the street again, closer and closer to where he stood, talking and sweeping, talking and sweeping always. Prayers she was reciting, surely, he smiled, but too proud to say them in public as the priests must have ordered her to. Yet the sweeping mystified him. There was something about it that made no sense. His brow furrowed. Why should she be sweeping the dust and debris of the street towards her own house, even into her own hallway? His forehead touched the part-opened shutters as he craned to hear her words. It creaked, ever so slightly. He froze. In the dawn silence it sounded to him as loud as the crackle of a dry axle. But Dame Alice gave no sign that she had heard, only continued sweeping intently. And now, as she passed just opposite where he stood in the greyness of half-light, he heard clearly what it was she said: 'To the house of William my son, come all the wealth of Kilkenny town.'

'To the house of William my son, come all the health of Kilkenny town.'

A strange prayer this, he thought, as he watched her hurry from view, off towards the far end of the street, where she again commenced her work. As before, she brushed, the rasping of the bristles and the buzz of her words making an eerie sound in the empty street. He shuddered. For the first time he noticed that he was cold. Without waiting to see her brush the last of the dust into her house, he turned to bed again, a chill about his heart that had nothing to do with the frostiness of the early morning air. He had witnessed something that had not been intended for his, or any other, eyes. Of that he was certain. He did not sleep again that morning.

In the weeks that followed it was noted by many of the good people of Kilkenny that all was not as it should be about the town. Curious happenings were afoot. Respectable businesses began to go bankrupt for no known reason; gold and valuables were found to have disappeared from safe hiding-places; even the beggars and the rats seemed to have forsaken the town. People began to feel a sense of gloom, as if something unwholesome, yet unseen, were hanging over them all.

Only one family seemed unaffected by all this: Alice Kyteler and her son, William. If anything, they seemed positively delighted with themselves, as if they knew something their fellow citizens did not. William, in ordinary times, was a wild young man who had so often brushed against the edges of the law that his friends called him William Outlawe; yet always he had been saved by his mother's influence and money. But now he took on a swagger that seemed to say to those who crossed his path, 'I am master of all I see — or soon will be!'

The rumours gathered again, thicker and darker than before. 'Witchcraft!' whispered the dank alleys. 'Devil's work!' hissed the cobblestones to any who had ears to hear. And there were many. The stealthy Art Artisson was seen ever more frequently by a populace that, strangely, began to be comforted as well as terrified by his shadowy presence.

In the midst of this state of affairs, Dame Alice's neighbour could no longer keep to himself the secret of what he had seen on May morning. No one now knows who first heard it from his lips, but certain it is that in the space of half a day the town was buzzing with the news. At last it came to the ears of the Mayor in his chamber in the Tholsel. He could well have done without this worry. A quarrel with someone as influential as Dame Kyteler was not a prospect he much relished. On the other hand, duty tugged at him. And the worst of all worlds would be gained by doing nothing; he was too long in politics not to realise that. Yet, in reality, there was little he could do ... except, maybe, to pass the problem to somebody more fitted to deal with it than he.

That is precisely what he did, and to none other than Richard de Ledrere, Bishop of Ossory. His lordship, an Englishman and a Franciscan, was disgusted, and angry, too, that he seemed to be the last person in his diocese to have heard of all this: 'Why have I been told nothing until now? Oh, this barbarous land!'

He paced the floor of his study, his jaws chewing on words silently. Uncomfortably the Mayor watched him, squeezing his cap all the while between his hands as though he were trying to wring invisible sweat out of it.

At last his lordship ceased his pacing and turned slowly, a determined look in his eyes. He faced the Mayor.

'You know what must be done!' he declared.

The Mayor did not, but he nodded — convincingly, he hoped. De Ledrere strode to his heavy oaken bench. From the jumble of scrolls there he took up a delicate silver bell and went to the door. Opening it with one hand, he rang the little instrument with a flick of the other — obviously a movement that was second nature to him. It tinkled into the gloom of the long corridor outside, and scarcely had its voice died away when before them stood a young man, dressed in the coarse garb of the brethren. In his hand were writing implements and fresh parchment. The Mayor had seen this man before: the Bishop's scribe. A man dexterous of hand

and quick of wit, no doubt. Richard de Ledrere had little space in his service for dullards, though he gladly gave alms to such of that ilk as accosted him in his travels. In many ways the Bishop was a strenuous follower of God's word. In the matter of witchcraft he was particularly so. Was it not written in *Deuteronomy* that none who practised the black arts were to be tolerated among the faithful? His duty was as clear as sight:

'Witches shall have no largeness of movement in Ossory so long as I am Bishop.'

He motioned the young man to the cluttered bench, swept clear a space with an impatient hand. 'Write thus,' he commanded...

Scarcely forty minutes later a messenger spurred a fast horse away from the Bishop's palace, in the direction of the Dublin road. In his pouch was the letter, and in his ears the Bishop's words still rang: 'Let no one — no one! — handle this missive save the Lord Chancellor himself.'

The messenger performed his duty precisely, though he was hardly thanked by those of the Chancellor's servants in Dublin Castle who regarded it as their privilege to shield his lordship from contact with mere vulgar countrymen. John d'Arcy read the Bishop's letter and growled. But only when the servant had been dismissed did he allow full vent to his feelings:

'This dolt, De Ledrere! Pig-headed friar. How dare he to level such accusations against Dame Alice. Well he knows she is my sister-in-law. But, this is designed to test me, to discover whether I will act. Curse that man, who puts me in such a plight!'

Whether Richard de Ledrere was deliberately trying to discredit the Lord Chancellor is not likely ever to be known, but the result was the same: from the day that the letter was delivered and read, the Bishop was a marked man. The Chancellor's spies dogged his steps whenever he left his house, and reports flowed to Dublin, where they were transformed into complaints, innuendo and abuse, all to the end that the Bishop might have few friends when the time of reckoning came.

That summer of 1324 he was called to the abbey of Kells to settle a question of disputed authority. He need not have gone. He might easily have ordered the clerical quarrellers to appear before him, but he had begun to be weary of Kilkenny and its oppressive air. A journey under God's blue sky would do much for his spirits. And so it was. He even managed to reconcile the combatants by a show of authority softened by *plámás* — ugly Irish word, but necessary, as so many others like it.

So now, here he was, after three days of what seemed to him a veritable holiday, riding south again, the plain of Meath sparkling on every side under a summer sun. He had hardly travelled a day's journey, however, when he was set upon by a band of low-looking villains. Against daggers and swords his servants' rosaries were of little avail. He was soon a prisoner.

A tall fellow, of ragged beard and pale complexion, seemed to be in command, for he it was who gave the orders. Now he stood boldly before the Bishop and with scant trace of respect sneered, 'So! You are the clever man who would have our mistress thrown in prison, eh? Well, let us see how you like it yourself, sir Bishop.'

And so they carried him off, deep into the forests of Meath, where he was chained securely and locked in a beggarly hut, fed on scraps and mocked without cease for nearly two weeks. But never once did his faith waver, or if it did he took good care to conceal the fact well. The only words he spoke were prayers for his poor benighted jailers, 'God's straying sheep', as he called them. At length, his prayers were answered, for one of the guards, less hardhearted than his companions, or moved, perhaps, by the Bishop's courage, set him free while the others slept, and even guided him through the forest paths, back to the public highway.

It was with some relief that his lordship entered the

gates of Kilkenny two days later, tired, bedraggled, but thankful for his escape. His troubles were far from over, however, did he but know it. After he had rested, his first act was to excommunicate Dame Alice and all who were associated with her in deeds of darkness, among them her son, William, and her servant, Petronilla de Meath. Publicly he did it, with bell, book and candle, in the presence of a huge crowd of the townspeople, who cheered his actions to the echo. Here at last was positive action from one who should know, and proof too that they themselves had not been mistaken in their opinion of the Dame.

The news was not greeted with such enthusiasm in Dublin Castle. John d'Arcy was beside himself. Like a man possessed he ranted, but this time almost as much against his indiscreet sister-in-law as against this scurvy Bishop who refused to leave well alone.

'Enough!' he shouted. 'This business has gone far enough, and shall be settled this very day.' He called his men, gave them gruff orders and sent them on their way towards Kilkenny.

Bishop de Ledrere had scarcely finished his evening prayers that day when a loud thumping of mailed fists and sword-hilts reached his ears from the direction of his front door. The servant who opened it was swept aside and, in a rush, a score of armed men entered his lordship's quarters. Dour-looking dogs they were, and all too plainly from Dublin, he thought. Their leader was abrupt, a man of small patience.

'You, sir, are the Lord Bishop of Ossory? Is such the case?'

'Yes. So I am called. But who, sir, are you? And why do you address me with such unfriendly looks?'

'Who we are matters not. You must come with us. Now! You are summoned. That is all.'

There was no arguing with such a fellow. Without so much as a change of clothing, he was hustled to Dublin, a prisoner for the second time in as many weeks. Vainly did he attempt to pry some information from his captors. Neither requests nor threats had the slightest effect. They rode on as men deaf and dumb; only their steely eyes, darting here and there, showed them for what they truly were.

More than one curious spectator paused to stare at the little cavalcade as it clattered through the streets of Dublin, but no one thought of it as anything more than the rich travelling in style, as usual. Nor did Richard de Ledrere complain any more. He was too occupied, casting over in his mind the words with which he would berate those who had so unceremoniously brought him here. But if he expected that he would be brought direct to the presence of his hidden enemy he was much mistaken. John d'Arcy had no intention of meeting him on equal terms. Better to test him first, let him see that obstinacy could be met with obstinacy. And so, the Bishop was taken to the nether regions of a strong house not far from the Castle, and pitched into a dungeon so dark that even when his eyes should have grown accustomed to the blackness, he could still see nothing. There he remained for seventeen days without warrant, never once spoken to by any living soul. Those who brought him his food were warned, under pain of torture, to speak to him never a syllable. And they obeyed.

He began to fear that he might not see the light of day again. 'Barbarous land. Barbarous people,' he muttered, not for the first time since coming to Ireland. But perhaps, there in the dark, the thought occurred to him occasionally that it was his own people, not the Irish, that he thus condemned. Certainly he was no fool, and the more he thought about his predicament and its possible causes, the closer came the finger of suspicion to John d'Arcy.

Whether it was his own prayers once more, or the exertions of his friends, he was not sure, but on the eighteenth day his cell door was thrown open and there stood the Chancellor, concern oozing from his fat jowls.

'My Lord Bishop!' he cried, 'Thank Heaven's mercy you

are well. Day and night have we searched ...

The Bishop was speechless. How could the fellow stand there, monstrously pretending to know nothing of what even a child could see he had himself ordered? Did he think those around him were feeble-minded? The light entering the cell was dim but to De Ledrere's eyes, so long deprived of the least ray, it had at first seemed like the flash of a midday sun. Now, though, as surprise rooted him before the still-prattling lord, he realised for the first time that someone else was there also. He peered. Surely ... it could not be ... his old friend, the Dean of St Patrick's. But it was. And his presence seemed little short of a miracle. He was on the point of asking how this could be, when, behind John d'Arcy's shoulder and unseen by him, the Dean laid a warning finger to his lips. Whatever the explanation for these events, it belonged to a more opportune time and place.

After a leisurely bath and a change of garments, the Bishop excused himself from all conversation with the Chancellor. He must pray, he said, thank God for his deliverance. Later that evening, by special invitation, he was summoned to the palace of the Archbishop, whose vicar general the Dean was, and there he learned of the happenings which had led to his release. His faithful scribe had followed at a discreet distance as his master had been led away, had noted their entry to Dublin Castle, their subsequent exit and going to the house nearby, and had guessed that something unpleasant was afoot. Vainly he had waited, day after day, for some sign, and when there was none he had at last come to the Archbishop's home, hardly daring to hope that he would even receive a hearing. But he had, and that most attentive, too, from the Dean, who was shocked to hear what the young man had to tell of happenings in Kilkenny. The Archbishop was informed at once, and his influence was the deciding factor. Not even the Lord Chancellor would dare to resist the power of such a man. And so his lordship's liberty had been procured.

But now it was De Ledrere's turn to speak. In scathing

terms (yet ever within the bounds of Christian charity), he described the late events. The Archbishop listened, attentive to every word, and the more he heard, the angrier he grew, until at last he would hear no more:

'So it has come to this! That a Bishop in his own diocese may no longer travel safely abroad, even in daytime, without being set upon by thieves, bandits and witches. But no longer! They have overstepped the bounds of good order and shall most assuredly answer for it. We fail grievously in our duty if we neglect to set a wholesome example.'

He ordered that a special court be convened in Kilkenny as soon as might be, to examine all those accused of witch-craft, and so diligently were his orders obeyed that not even John d'Arcy could shelter Dame Alice this time. In fact, he was himself fortunate to escape with only a censure.

Richard de Ledrere returned to Kilkenny to a hero's welcome. Crowds lined the road into the town, and the ancient streets were thronged with cheering men, women and children. Flowers were thrown at him and green branches laid in his path. He was home, and he was victorious. But though he waved his thanks to his people, he knew who it was that had brought him safely through his ordeal. So, without even pausing at his own house, he went straight to St Canice's Cathedral, there to offer his gratitude for his good fortune. The multitude followed him in a huge procession, everyone in a high good humour, and the walls of the ancient church rang that day to the sound of hymns of joy.

An even greater cause of satisfaction to the Bishop was the fact that all three of the accused had been arrested without delay — Dame Alice, her son William and Petronilla. They were now lodged in Kilkenny jail, awaiting the arrival of a Judge from Dublin. Within a week he came, a severe-looking man, bald of head and ample of girth — the perfect combination, it was agreed, for a man of learning. He set the trial-date, ordered that a jury be enrolled, then betook himself to his private rooms, shunning the company of all, even the Bishop.

On the day appointed, the law-court was packed almost to suffocation. Everyone of importance in the town was there, particularly those who supposed they had suffered losses or injury through the dark deeds of the accused. Excitement rose in that sweating room, and with it a buzz of conversation that was stilled at last only by the entry of the Judge. The usual formalities were soon disposed of and the moment arrived that all had been looking forward to, the bringing in of the prisoners. One by one they came, each flanked by two guards. They had not been allowed to change their attire for this appearance, a circumstance that caused no little surprise, for few of the spectators had ever seen Dame Alice other than in fine array. But though her clothing was less than lovely now, she still possessed her pride. Head high, she walked to her seat and settled herself, seemingly unconcerned. Not so Petronilla. She was frightened, and she showed it. With William it was harder to tell, so bedraggled had he become. A thrill ran through the packed benches. It had all the prospect of being a trial of the utmost interest.

At a signal from the Judge, a clerk stood forth, unrolled a bulky parchment and began to read. Every ear strained to catch the words: 'Dame Alice Kyteler, inasmuch as you have dabbled in those things that rightly are hid from the knowing of men's minds, and thereby transgressed against the laws of God and of this realm, you are here enjoined to give account of yourself, that the powers spiritual and temporal may be satisfied.' There followed a long catalogue of the crimes she was accused of, a most impressive list, if judged by the reaction of the crowd. At each new 'revelation' a burst of whispering cut across the clerk's words, only to subside as the next charge was read.

'Well, madam,' said the Judge when the clerk had ended, 'what is your defence against these heinous accusations?'

She answered him not a single word, and no matter what questions were levelled at her thereafter, she haughtily refused to make reply or to defend herself in any way. She never moved, except to rake the assembled people with her cold eyes.

'Very well, madam,' said the Judge. 'Perhaps we may yet bend your stubborn will. Bring in the witness!'

The crowd's excitement bubbled up again as the witness — none other than her neighbour — was directed to the witness-bench, where he sat uncomfortably, in full view of the accused. It was obvious to all that he was nervous, even afraid, but now that the slow wheels of justice had begun to turn, they could no longer be halted. At the Judge's request, he began to tell what he had witnessed that May morning, watched all the time by the hard eyes of Dame Kyteler. Under that unswerving glare he began to stumble in his words and several times had to be called to order by the severe voice of his lordship: 'Stop! Repeat what you have even now said. And cease your mutterings. Scarcely can I hear what you say.'

The poor man did his best, squirming and sweating all the while. 'Your honour, she said words like, "To the house of William my son come all the health of Kilkenny town". She said that while she brushed the street to her door.'

The murmur from the crowd began again, louder than before, but all was stilled on Bishop de Ledrere's sudden rising from his chair in the front row.

'Aye,' he cried, 'and many a person there is in this town who can truly swear that her evil devices have since come to fruit.'

Much nodding of heads in the room showed the Judge that this was indeed so. He turned once more to the accused.

'Lady, it were better for you presently to answer to these charges. Else you stand in mortal danger.'

Yet she answered not a syllable.

The Judge was becoming impatient now. He reached beneath his bench, held up a square of black cloth.

'You must know what this signifies.'

If she did she gave no sign. He continued.

'Force not my hand, madam, for if once I pronounce you witch, your doom is sealed. Admit to your evil-doing while yet you may. Then perhaps may you be admitted to mercy and forgiveness.'

It was a fair plea on his part, clearly in deference to her rank. A lesser person — or maybe one more guilty — would have grasped the opportunity willingly. But not Dame Alice. Her only acknowledgement that she had even heard his words was a slight smile.

Scarcely able to hide his irritation, the Judge, very deliberately, so that all might see, placed the black cloth on his head.

'So be it,' he said grimly. And thus he pronounced his sentence: that the prisoner be brought forth from the jail one week from that day, and taken to the place of public execution, there to receive the full rigours of the law.

A like sentence was passed on Petronilla by the angry Judge, despite all her protests of innocence. The jury was hardly even necessary. But William was not condemned to death. He denied knowing anything of his mother's wicked deeds; more than that, he condemned her in no uncertain terms and promised compensation to all citizens who might claim it. He begged forgiveness of Bishop de Ledrere for any injury he might have done him, and promised, on pain of forfeiture of all he possessed, to be of good behaviour thereafter.

The Bishop was unimpressed by this sudden conversion; to him it seemed too much like a drowning man snatching at any straw that might save him. But the Judge was more favourably disposed, no doubt because that morning he had received a letter from the Treasurer himself in Dublin, inquiring after the health of 'my good friend, William'. He ordered that the capital charges be dropped, but levied a fine of five hundred marks instead, half of it payable to the Dublin Treasury, the rest to be used to purchase lead for the roof of St Canice's Cathedral, which of late had begun urgently to need repairs. Not even the Bishop could argue with that. After all, it would spare his flock the unpleasing task of delving into their purses. But, little did he realise that William Outlawe would fulfil his obligation only too well.

The court's business done, the guards were summoned and ordered to take the prisoners to the dungeons. Dame Alice was hauled roughly to her feet. 'Come, madam. Your lodgings await.' But before they could take her away she shot out a threatening finger at her neighbour and spoke her only words of all that day's proceedings: 'Think not, neighbour, that you will see my death a week hence,' and then to the crowd, 'No, nor any one of ye who came today to see this sport.'

Before another word could cross her lips, she was dragged off, Petronilla also, to the condemned cell, leaving behind them a hush where a hundred voices had babbled moments before.

The condemned cell of Kilkenny jail was not built with comfort in mind. Its thick stone walls were dank even on the hottest summer day, and the sun never shone on its cold floor. The little barred window high in the wall saw to that. Furniture there was none, except a single three-legged stool, and the only bed was a bundle of musty straw in one corner. It was a place that had saddened the heart of many a poor wretch in his last days on this green earth. Now Dame Alice and Petronilla were bundled in, the iron door clanged behind them and they were alone, save for the guards, who would now pace the corridor outside twenty-four hours a day, until the moment of execution.

Those who had been present at the trial scattered, some to the taverns, others to their homes, all to relive the day's happenings. The neighbour who had borne witness was not a drinking man, and after a short conversation with the Bishop, he hurried direct to his own place, hardly daring to glance at where William Outlawe already stood at the window of his mother's house. Having carefully locked and bolted his outer door, the man went to his private chamber, fell on his knees and begged the saints' protection against all evil.

That evening he had his supper at the usual hour and retired early to bed. But in the dead hours of the night he awoke suddenly with a scream. Pain after piercing pain stabbed through his stomach and chest, as though he were being attacked with knives by many unseen hands. His shrieks awakened the servants. They rushed to his side, crying, 'Master! Master! Heaven save us, what ails you?'

'Their knives ... they stab me! Help me! Protect me, I beg ye.'

'Who, master? Whose knives?'

'Alice Kyteler and her crew of spotted fiends! A priest, friends, and a doctor, in God's name. Quickly!'

Those gentlemen were routed from their beds and speedily conveyed to his bedside, but the doctor could do nothing and the priest little more; the poor man never saw the light of another day. He died, his eyes wide with terror, as if looking into the face of the Beast himself.

If Dame Alice knew anything of all this, she was not prepared to talk about it, though she was repeatedly questioned. And so the days dragged by. But as one followed another the relief of recent times seemed to evaporate and a sinister presence again was felt to clutch the town. Nervously, the people counted away the hours, until finally, on the morning of the fatal day, the Mayor stepped forth from the Tholsel, dressed in all his splendid robes. On his heels followed Richard de Ledrere, also arrayed for the occasion, and, were it not for his presence, the Mayor would have refused point-blank to perform his sworn duty, come of it what might. Even now, his hand shook slightly as he began to unroll the parchment on which was written the mortal proclamation.

There were few of the citizens gathered to watch him as he read. Only the bravest had ventured out, though many more stood discreetly behind closed doors and shutters, straining to hear his measured words. He began: 'Be it known to all that I, by the grace of God Mayor of this town of Kilkenny, do hereby order, in the name of the powers spiritual and temporal of this kingdom, that Dame Alice Kyteler and Petronilla of Meath be brought forth and conveyed to the place of execution, that the sentence of the court may be carried out. Guards! Bring forth Petronilla of Meath!'

The guards clanked into the dark interior of the jail, ordered the jailer to give up the prisoner. 'Prepare yourself, Dame Kyteler,' they gibed as they led the wretched servant out. But Alice paid them not the slightest heed, only gazed intently at the barred window, as if meditating.

Pale as death Petronilla was, but through all her ordeal she would never once cry for mercy or speak ill of her mistress. They led her to where the stakes stood like the doorjambs of eternity, and bound her quickly and securely. A spark, a wisp of smoke, and in a few moments the flames were crackling through the dry wood piled around, feeling their hungry way towards her. To the very limit of human endurance she clenched her teeth and suffered in silence, but at last she could bear it no further, and her agonised screams echoed through the narrow streets, re-echoed from the walls of St Canice's Cathedral, and off across the pleasant waters of the Nore. Many a secret listener shuddered, hearing in her awful shrieks the terror of a lost soul falling into eternal darkness. Others, more fastidious, felt a twinge of disgust at the barbarousness of the proceedings — could she not merely have been kept in jail, where she would speedily be forgotten about, as many another had?

Soon enough, Petronilla's hard passage from this world was over. Only the smell of cooking flesh lingered on in the still air for some time longer while the fire was allowed to burn itself into embers. Some of those who watched could not help but pray. Petronilla had been no stranger to them. Had they not met her almost daily, hurrying about her mistress' business in the town? Or seen her, head bowed, praying in the cathedral of a Sunday? A few had even known her well. Now she was dead. Most horribly dead.

Their thoughts were interrupted by the Mayor's voice. He was reading in his official tone, the self-same words again. Only the ending was different: '... Guards! Bring forth Alice Kyteler.'

Once more those wooden-faced men tramped off to do his bidding. The Captain in command was first to shoulder his arrogant way into the jail. He was still striding ahead when they entered the dim corridor to the condemned cell. Then, almost before he became aware even of doing it, he was grimacing, running his forefinger between the top of his heavy leathern cuirass and his neck. It was cursedly warm here, he thought, his mind still lagging behind, not taking in the significance of what his senses told him. He was roused from his abstraction by a growl from behind: 'God's mercy, this place must be afire!' Like a whiplash, the Captain moved, thought and action combining in a fraction of a second. He sprang towards the iron cell door, grasped the

136

great handle, but leaped back even more quickly, shrieking and cursing, leaving the skin of his fingers behind. The door was red hot! Even as he sank to his knees, squeezing his injured hand to his side, he was pouring out a string of oaths mixed with orders: to fetch buckets, bring water and throw it on the door. Weapons were hurriedly cast aside, and a human chain formed in that narrow place. Yet it was five long minutes before the first bucket of water appeared and was flung against the metal. A blast of steam billowed out with a loud hiss, hiding the door from view, almost choking them.

'More! More! Speedily!' shouted the Captain above the confused din. Several buckets more were directed at the same surface, until at last it could be seen that there was a lessening of the heat. Only then did they pause and approach for a closer look. Yet no man dared to be the first to risk his hand by touching.

'Come, fools!' snarled the Captain. 'The Mayor awaits.' 'You sergeant! Make trial of the lock. Find whether the door may be opened.'

The burly man obeyed, though reluctantly. He could see all too clearly how things stood with the Captain's own hand, and he had no wish to share in his sufferings. He snapped a quick salute, pulled on his gauntlet and reached out gingerly. To his great relief all was once again normal — or almost. The handle, the door itself, were burned black. He attempted to draw back the heavy bolts, but strain as he might, they stirred not a fraction of an inch. Nor could two men together do better. Nor three.

At that moment a voice sounded over the sweaty straining and grunting of the group. A messenger from the Mayor.

'In God's name, Captain, what delays you? His Worship awaits, and the Lord Bishop.'

Mouthing a curse, the Captain hurried to acquaint him with their problem, barking as he went, 'Ho, there, some of you. Find us a smith! Tell him to bring with him his weight-

iest sledge-hammer. Go! At once!'

The blacksmith, a heavy-set man, lame of foot, came unwillingly. Like many another, he had been content to witness this day's doings from a safe distance. Now here he was, active at their very centre.

The Lord Bishop was becoming most impatient. That much, at least, was made clear to the Captain, so his orders to the smith were short and sharp: 'Your best strokes, fellow! Smash down this door.'

They stood back as he eyed the metal shrewdly, then balanced himself firmly on his good leg. The clash of his first stroke made them jump. They were more nervous than they would have dared to admit. No one spoke as the thunderous blows continued to fall expertly, rhythmically, and out into the listening streets came the harshness of his hammer, to the ears of those who sat hidden from view, and likewise to those who huddled before the Mayor, shiftily surveying the smouldering remains of Petronilla.

Richard de Ledrere could take no more. 'God's blood,' he swore, 'what hellish noise is this?' He swung impatiently from the Mayor's side, strode towards the jail. He would have an answer, now, or others besides Dame Kyteler would suffer!

An answer of sorts was already to hand, for at that instant the smith's great hammer connected a last time with the stubborn metal. Of a sudden, one of the iron hinges sprang from the massive jamb and the door slewed drunkenly inward. With a yell of triumph, the soldiers surged forward into the little chamber, weapons at the ready. They were unnecessary. The cell was empty of all but the charred remnants of the stool and a handful of smouldering straw in its corner. Of Alice Kyteler there was nothing. They darted fearful glances hither and thither, each man too taken aback to speak. Up along the walls, almost to the stone ceiling, their eyes followed scorch marks and the stains of smoke. The Captain pointed to the window. It was obvious that he was confused. 'How could ...?' He never finished the question. There was no need. The answer was all too obvious, for the iron bars were still securely in place. Nobody had gone that way; so much was clear to them all.

'The Bishop! Bring the Bishop at once!' hissed the Captain, his eyes still firmly fixed on that impossible window. 'If he can answer this ...' He was interrupted by a commotion in the corridor, and a hurried, respectful drawing back of bodies. Richard de Ledrere it was, impatience and anger written large in his face.

'Who commands here?' he snapped, and without waiting for a reply, 'Where is the prisoner? Why has she not been brought forth?'

The Captain faced him. An insane urge to smirk almost overcame him as he replied, 'Perchance your Lordship can answer such a question. My humble self cannot.'

The Bishop was visibly taken aback. He looked about him, at the helpless, bewildered soldiers' faces, at the slightly hostile Captain, at the walls, the window. The smell of smoke was in his nostrils as his mind fumbled for words adequate to explain the strange sight. All eyes were on him, curious, expectant. Long years of preaching on hellfire and damnation now came to his assistance, and he began, haltingly at first, but with growing confidence. His anger had dissolved. Here was God's will indeed, witnessed by these, His faithful. Who could deny the evidence of his own eyes? He spoke on, even though his mind was diverted by many possibilities and suppositions: '... and so, brethren, it seems to me none other than that the Old One has come for her at last. A true saying it is that the devil knows his own...'

Heads nodded in agreement. Yes, that was it, surely. The Bishop had the rights of it. They were satisfied, and proud in a way, to have been of some small service in the great work of salvation.

The Bishop had another reason to be thankful, too, for as he walked back to his house, he recalled William Outlawe's fine, and the new roof that would soon adorn St Canice's Cathedral. He determined to remind Outlawe of his obligation that very day. Much to his surprise, however, William needed no reminding; he even provided twice the stipulated amount of lead and, moreover, personally supervised its laying on, a circumstance that caused some scratching of heads, raising of eyebrows.

'Perhaps he *was* ignorant of his mother's evildoing', became the general comment in Kilkenny's streets and taverns, though some few doubters (the Bishop included) shook their heads, muttered, 'like mother, like son'. Perhaps William's intentions were worthy, yet the sceptics could at least indulge in quiet, knowing smiles when on 22 May 1332, a large part of the cathedral collapsed under the dead weight of the lead. Faulty building? Or Alice Kyteler's last laugh at those who had interrupted her secret business?

Perhaps Richard de Ledrere could once again have ventured an answer. But by then he had moved on to higher places and better things.

GLOSSARY

Amadán:	A fool.
Bodach:	A stupid, ignorant person.
Bothán:	A miserable little house.
A bhuachaill:	Boy. Affectionate interjection.
Cailleach:	A hag, an old woman.
Claíomh:	A sword.
A Chríost is a Mhuire Mháthair:	Christ and Mary his Mother. Interjection.
A chroí:	My darling. Affectionate interjection.
Dailtín:	A low fellow.
In ainm Dé:	In God's name.
Meitheal:	A gang of workmen.
A mhic:	Son. Affectionate interjection.
Mná feasa:	Wise women.
An modh díreach:	The most direct way of doing something.
Omós:	Honour, respect.
Plámás:	Flattery, soft talk.
Seisiún:	A session. Most often a musical gathering.
Síbín:	An illicit drinking-house.
Sprus:	Rubbish. Contemptuous term for persons of no account.

MORE MERCIER BESTSELLERS

STRANGE IRISH TALES FOR CHILDREN
Edmund Lenihan

Strange Irish Tales for Children is a collection of four hilarious stories, by seanchaí Edmund Lenihan, which will entertain and amuse children of all ages.

The stories tell of the adventures of the Fianna and about Fionn MacCumhail's journey to Norway in search of a blackbird. There is a fascinating tale about 'The Strange Case of Seán na Súl' whose job was to kidnap people to take them away to a magic island. 'Taoscán MacLiath and the Magic Bees' is a story about the exploits of this very famous druid and about how he packed his spell-books and took himself off to the conference held by the druids of the Seven Lands.

STORIES OF OLD IRELAND FOR CHILDREN
Edmund Lenihan

Long ago in Ireland there were men who used to travel to the four ends of the earth and few travelled farther than Fionn and the men of the Fianna during their many exciting adventures. In *Stories of Old Ireland for Children* we read about 'Fionn Mac Cumhail and Feathers of China', 'King Cormac's Fighting Academy', and 'Fionn and the Mermaids'.

TALES OF IRISH ENCHANTMENT
Patricia Lynch

Patricia Lynch brings to this selection of classical Irish folktales for young people all the imagination and warmth for which she is renowned.

There are seven stories here: Midir and Etain, The Quest of the Sons of Turenn, The Swan Children, Deirdre and the Sons of Usna, Labra the Mariner, Cuchulain – The Champion of Ireland and The Voyage of Maeldun.

They lose none of their original appeal in the retelling and are as delightful today as when they were first told.

The stories are greatly enhanced by the immediacy and strength of Frances Boland's imaginative drawings.

ENCHANTED IRISH TALES
Patricia Lynch

Enchanted Irish Tales tells of ancient heroes and heroines, fantastic deeds of bravery, magical kingdoms, weird and wonderful animals... This new illustrated edition of classical folktales, retold by Patricia Lynch with all the imagination and warmth for which she is renowned, rekindles the age-old legends of Ireland, as exciting today as they were when first told. The collection includes:

- Conary Mór and the Three Red Riders
- The Long Life of Tuan Mac Carrell
- Finn Mac Cool and Fianna
- Oisin and The Land of Youth
- The Kingdom of The Dwarfs
- The Dragon Ring of Connla
- Mac Datho's Boar
- Ethne